# JOURNEY
### through
# ASTROLOGY

'Ultimately astrology is not a technique but an initiation into a way of life which, because of its mysterious familiarity, often feels like a coming home.'

CLARE MARTIN,
*MAPPING THE PSYCHE*, VOL.1

# JOURNEY through ASTROLOGY

CHARTING THE ASTROLOGICAL VOYAGE OF DISCOVERY

*Edited by*
Laura Andrikopoulos, Cat Cox
and Carole Taylor

FACULTY OF
ASTROLOGICAL STUDIES
PRESS

Copyright © Faculty of Astrological Studies 2015

Copyright © Individual chapter copyright is held jointly between the individual contributor and the Faculty of Astrological Studies 2015

All rights reserved. No part of this publication may be reproduced, stored in a retrieval system, or transmitted in any form or by any means, electronic, mechanical, photocopying, recording or otherwise, without the prior permission in writing from the copyright owner.

The Faculty of Astrological Studies has asserted its right to be identified as the author of this work.

First published in 2015 by the Faculty of Astrological Studies

The Faculty of Astrological Studies
BCM Box 7470
London WC1N 3XX
England, UK
Tel: 07000 790143
www.astrology.org.uk
facultypress@astrology.org.uk

A CIP catalogue record for this book
is available from the British Library
ISBN 978-0-9932-7670-5

Cover and book design www.eamessurman.com
Book set in Centaur 11pt and Gill Sans Light

Cover image: Harley 4431 f. 189v British Library www.bl.uk

Editors: Laura Andrikopoulos, Cat Cox and Carole Taylor
Printed by IngramSpark

# CONTENTS

| | |
|---|---|
| Introduction | 7 |
| Acknowledgements | 9 |
| 1 The Initial Awakening<br>CAT COX | 11 |
| 2 The Art of Interpretation<br>CAROLE TAYLOR | 25 |
| 3 Negotiating the Future<br>KIM FARLEY | 41 |
| 4 Becoming Your Own Astrologer<br>POLLY WALLACE | 54 |
| 5 Perils and Pitfalls on the Path: Ethics in<br>Astrological Practice<br>DEBORAH MORGAN | 69 |
| 6 Engaging and Dialoguing with Another Person<br>in an Astrological Consultation<br>LINDSAY RADERMACHER | 84 |
| 7 Living an Astrological Philosophy: Astrology<br>as Guide and Spiritual Practice<br>DIANE CONWAY | 99 |
| 8 Astrology in the Modern World<br>LAURA ANDRIKOPOULOS | 114 |
| 9 My Life in Astrology<br>DARBY COSTELLO | 130 |
| 10 A Life Astrological<br>MELANIE REINHART | 145 |
| Authors' Biographies | 162 |
| Bibliography | 165 |
| List of Illustrations | 169 |
| About the Faculty of Astrological Studies | 170 |

'...astrologers are driven by an intellectual quest, a need to find some kind of cosmic order which can give meaning, if not an answer, to the mystery of human suffering. This is where we see the Centaur at work, for in myth he is not only a healer – he is a philosopher-sage and a teacher of astrology.'

LIZ GREENE,
THE ASTROLOGER, THE COUNSELLOR AND THE PRIEST

# INTRODUCTION

THE FACULTY PRESS has been long in gestation. Founded in 1948, the Faculty of Astrological Studies has been dedicated to excellence in astrological education for over sixty-five years and has been committed to providing each successive generation with sufficient training to understand the central elements of astrological theory and practice. It has achieved this by developing a rigorous set of courses and examinations, designed to ensure that its prestigious Diploma is gained only by those who are truly dedicated to their astrological studies and craft. Over the years, the Faculty has published a few works, yet, in contrast to this book, these have been of the nature of teaching material, often concerned with the practical skills and techniques of astrological interpretation.

What then makes this book so different? We believe this current work is unique amongst the currently available astrology-related publications, for this work is not concerned with techniques or interpretation but addresses the inner experience of the astrological journey. It interweaves the personal reflections of the authors with their specific chapter theme.

We might say that Venus had a hand in this book. In the Faculty's chart, Venus lies retrograde in Cancer in the 8th house. Her gentle, mysterious and deep beauty is turned inward, away from the outside world. To find her you must first penetrate the outer shell – commit to a rigorous process of study and examination. This might make it seem as though enrolling as an astrology student were just like enrolling for any other course. But this is far from the case.

Those on the inside of the Faculty, who are part of the Faculty family – our students, tutors, Council, alumni, patrons and friends throughout the international astrological community – well understand both its inner and outer beauty. But there are many who may not quite understand the nature of the subject they are attracted to, and who believe that they can easily gain knowledge and qualifications in astrology just as with more conventional subjects, without substantial inner change. The outside of the Faculty and other astrological schools may speak of rigour, taxing examinations and qualifications but the inner story of astrology, the finding, learning, loving, despairing of it but then falling in love with it over again, and living it, is one that is not so easily captured by a formal educational process. Yet it is there, awaiting discovery, awaiting communication.

And so, as Pluto in Capricorn opposed the Faculty's Venus, the Faculty Council explored and debated the question of how to transform the inner beauty of the journey through astrology into tangible form. This book is the result. We hope you will enjoy its

8th house Venus in Cancer flavour: the joy of finding astrology and its esoteric secrets, of being captivated and bewitched by its numinous archetypal allure, of developing one's own relationship to its mysterious and sometimes maddeningly irrational components. In this book, the journey through astrology awaits you, the journey that each who is called to deeply enter the heart of this ancient practice must take.

The book consists of ten chapters, each written by a different author. The first eight chapters each seek to explore some aspect of the journey through astrology whilst the final two offer reflections on their lives in astrology from two of the world's most respected astrologers: Darby Costello and Melanie Reinhart.

Chapter one explores the initial awakening, that process of becoming acquainted with astrology for the first time, the realisation that one has stumbled upon something of momentous import. This can be a rather jolting experience, as the world around one begins to appear somewhat different and the symbolic mode of perception starts to awaken. Chapters two, three, and four describe the process of learning to interpret astrological symbolism and horoscopes, of grappling with the issue of forecasting, and of really starting to become one's own astrologer.

With chapter five we move to a consideration of the ethics of astrological knowledge and practice, of navigating the perils and pitfalls that could await the budding practitioner. Chapter six goes on to explore how the astrological experience may be shared with another through the medium of a consultation or reading, and the journey that accompanies that sharing.

The question of integrating astrology into one's spiritual journey forms the basis of the richly poetic chapter seven, whilst in chapter eight we consider the realities of astrology's place in the modern world and how each person who makes the journey through astrology comes to terms with being a citizen of two seemingly discordant worldviews.

The joys and sacrifices of a life in astrology are recalled in the final two chapters of the book, as we travel with Darby and Melanie on their own journeys.

We have dedicated this book to the student of astrology. It is for all who are journeying through various stages of their astrological lives.

Laura Andrikopoulos, Cat Cox and Carole Taylor
March 2015

# ACKNOWLEDGEMENTS

Like the Faculty itself, this book is the result of collaborative effort. It has been inspired by the thousands of students taught by the Faculty over the decades, each undergoing his or her own particular journey through astrology and adding to the sum total of knowledge and understanding of this most precious and illuminating subject.

The Faculty is run by a Council, made up of tutoring Diploma holders, and it is to the Council that the Faculty owes a debt of thanks in helping to bring this book to fruition. At time of publication, the Council consists of President Laura Andrikopoulos, Vice-President and Head Tutor Cat Cox, Council Secretary and Finance Officer Deborah Morgan, Director of Studies and Summer School Organiser Carole Taylor, Advertising Officer Stevi Gaydon, and Council members Penny de Abreu, Lindsay Gladstone and Clair Bentley, with Head of Exams Glòria Roca as a non-Council officer.

We are also indebted to Penny de Abreu for her role as sub-editor – Penny's proofreading skills have long been an asset with regard to the production of our course material and her work on the manuscript has been invaluable.

## Chapter One
# THE INITIAL AWAKENING
### CAT COX

Travelling home one autumn night in West London in 1984, after one of my first astrology classes, I was transfixed by a row of London plane trees whose canopies of leaves silhouetted against the dark sky were sparkling with a brilliant radiance. Animated by arcs of light radiating through the branches they were streaming with energy, creating a glittering aura of illumination which bathed each tree in a magical glow. In that enchanting moment I had a sense of the world coming awake and of something mysterious and hitherto unknown revealing itself to me, as if presented with a glimpse into another world.

I had found my way to Sue Tompkins' beginners' astrology class in Hammersmith in September of that year at a time of a wealth of Adult Education classes run under the auspices of the Greater London Authority. For as long as I could remember I had been interested in astrology, magic and the path of the Mysteries and now, at a point in life with a university degree just completed but with no apparently clear idea of what direction to take or what lay ahead, I had just taken a significant step in joining this class.

A series of events and experiences swiftly unfolded from those first beginnings; an introduction to the tarot came through another astrology student, a series of remarkable synchronicities unfolded and some significant meetings took place which later led to an inspiration to travel and explore the wider world. I had become fascinated and enthralled with this new study. I was busy tracking the planetary movements, actively looking at the world through this new ordering system of planetary correspondences and I was beginning to read the world through this new framework of meaning. And at this point too I began the lifelong practice of following the planetary transits to my chart and observing the cycles in the outer world and their corollary in inner life. I was starting to pay attention to the cycles of time weaving around me which were most apparent in the lunar cycle enacted across the heavens on a monthly basis from silver crescent to luminous full moon and diminishing light on the waning tide. I tentatively related this then to the annual seasonal changes in a practice which deepened in psychological and mythic understanding some years later as I began to ritualise the Wheel of the Year, observing these cycles of ebb and flow in nature and discovering these patterns reflected in my own inner life experience. Time was becoming a cyclical path rather than a linear trajectory.

I recognised that astrology was both deeply satisfying to my intellectual need for meaning in life and also profoundly experiential as I began to realise that the symbols I was so fascinated by in the chart on the page or in the ephemeris were arising around me in outer events as lived and living experience. I was finding my way into a new relationship with the world that was meaningful and reciprocal and connected in ways that were hitherto unknown to me and seemingly unrecognised in mainstream culture around me. My relationship to life and the cosmos was changing and I was being pulled to explore this new landscape more deeply.

### SHARED NARRATIVES

Elements of this narrative may be a familiar story to many who find themselves drawn to astrology or who find in astrology a sense of homecoming. In conversations with fellow astrologers who have shared with me their journey into astrology, a number of similar themes emerge.[1] From excitement and thrill on first making the discovery, the astrological journey leads to endless fascination with the connections and meaning that arise in this new way of relating to life. For many, magical meetings and synchronicities abound as we first find astrology, reinforcing a sense of something mysterious stirring. And as we embark on this mysterious adventure new interests may follow with other magical or divinatory practices such as working with tarot, or making a deep connection with the moon and the night sky, or exploring sacred space, or ritualising the seasonal cycles and these can run as byways alongside this call to astrology.

Some astrologers describe a sense of coming home as they arrive into astrology which may be experienced in the joy and embodied sense of pleasure of working with a chart or in the nourishment from a wider sense of existing in a meaningful world; others share the importance of a deep connection with nature, where participative experiences of the world have arisen in moments of enchantment; and some astrologers describe a sense of entering a relationship with this new way of experiencing and being in the world where astrology is to be responded to and worked with rather than something to be objectively learned.

Whilst for some people the journey into astrology appears to be gentle and slow, for others connection with astrology seems to brings big life changes in its wake, reordering the pre-existing life into a new form or redirecting it onto a new path, yet within this disruption there is a sense of beginning to find meaning in these life changes as the astrologer's worldview slowly shifts and a sense of meaning in the restructuring of life is glimpsed. Some astrologers have referred to the experience of synchronicities and patterns of correspondences bringing a magical thread into life and the universe seeming 'different', of seeing that there is a pattern at work, perhaps realising that there is some kind of shape to what is arising. The new-found perception of pattern and shape intimates that there may be some meaning to life experiences. A meaningful sense of structure of the cosmos and the life lived within it begins to emerge, where astrological insight helps to make sense of the shape and pattern of events and changes. As one astrologer shared with me, 'Life was becoming apparent as a process, imbued with meaning available by referring what was happening back to the symbol – a symbol that would make sense and from which one is then able to see a wider pattern'.

A repeating theme in these early beginnings of finding one's way into astrology is a growing awareness of a felt understanding of being connected in ways hitherto unrecognised or unknown, where 'everything corresponds to everything else', and all things are linked together by invisible relationships between them. These invisible webs of connections seem to the astrologer to extend throughout the whole world creating an intangible framework that encompasses the whole of life experience such that one can recognise that, both in the world around one and in the interior of one's own life, a process is unfolding, and that there is a dimension of meaning present which is there even if it cannot be physically seen or rationally understood. For as another astrologer reflected, 'Things don't just happen; there is an order to it even if I can't see it is there'.

A dominant thread running through narratives of the path into astrology is an awareness of coming to see life and the life journey in terms of cycles. Changes arising can be correlated with and characterised by a connection with cyclical patterns, encompassing cycles of personal development, cycles in nature and a growing sense of things developing in their own meaningful time. Alongside becoming aware of the planetary cycles through the ephemeris, for some astrologers their ongoing relationship with the sky or through different kinds of embodied or spiritual practice, grounds the awareness and enhances the ability to see cycles in operation such that one starts to observe matters waxing and waning in tandem with the ebb and flow of cyclical time. With a growing awareness of patterns in the sky being mirrored in life, where cycles moving 'above' are reflected in matters evolving 'below', these symbolic patterns of time become not just intellectually understood but increasingly embedded in lived experience with a sense of 'rhythm and pace and unfolding'.

Another narrative in the astrological journey is a sense of beginning to develop a relationship with astrology. Moving from a relationship of independent and detached observer of the world, a perception develops that one is in some kind of dialogue or partnership with the cosmos. And infusing this two-way flow there is a perception that astrology itself has its own agency. In entering this relationship the astrologer might begin to explore how to work with it, or have a sense of how to be guided by it and taught by it, and can develop a commitment to it such that our journey into astrology takes us into a relationship with astrology itself. Indeed for many astrologers over time the relationship with astrology can become a constant thread in life. And from its early beginnings it can become so deeply woven into the fibre of life so as to become unimaginable how to view the world without this frame.

## CORRESPONDENCES

One of the ways that we start to see patterns arising around us in the world and begin to develop a framework of meaning is through the understanding of planetary correspondences. These are the great webs of symbolic connection linking a planet to the multiplicity of attributes both material and psychological with which it is associated. As a key tenet of hermetic philosophy, the principle of correspondences has a long history extending back through Renaissance and Medieval philosophy. Linking heaven and earth as in the ancient axiom of 'as above, so below', these are the great invisible, acausal, symbolic relationships between the planets in the heavens and the myriad things in our world that each planet corresponds to.

As we enter astrology one of the first things we learn is to categorise all things under the sun to a planetary power and then we start to watch for and recognise this planetary symbolism in astrological signatures arising in the world around us. As an image to support our learning we might imagine a great wooden filing cabinet with rows of labelled draws assigned to each planet into which the whole cosmos can be filed under its corresponding planet; from plants and herbs to day-to-day objects, to qualities, events and psychological states each correlating with one planet and allied then to the planet's symbolic meaning. Over time we train ourselves to recognise these planetary correlations as we learn the meaning of the planets and find our way around our filing system; we then pay attention as we notice objects, events or experiences calling our attention in the world around us thereby showing the planet in play and we are able to translate this into planetary meaning. We might have found ourselves caught up in the pomp and grandeur of a royal pageant and recognise the regal symbolism of the Sun enacted around us, or we witness a sudden display of violent temper and know this to be choler-laden Mars, or making our way through the backstreets of the old quarter of a city a gate in an archway remains stubbornly closed and we link this to Saturn who symbolises boundaries well held or delays along our path or the finality of endings. At times we might find that this planetary symbolism carries deeper meaning for us: pipes burst or the bath overflows and we have a flood in the house and recognise Neptune at work and link this to a lack of boundaries in another area of life; the choleric expression out in the street alerts us to our own anger at a challenging situation in our personal life; the door remaining obstinately shut may carry meaning for us of a closure or ending in a different part of life or reflect our own interior sense of feeling resistant or constrained.

## SYNCHRONICITY

The term synchronicity was first coined by Carl Jung to describe such juxtaposed events and experiences where the events are not linked through cause and effect but the coincidence of the events is striking and meaningful to the participant. There is an inner and outer component to the 'meaningful coincidence' where the outer event offers a parallel to the inner psychic awareness, yet these inner and outer events are not themselves causally related.[2] Crucially it is the powerful experience of the sense of meaning in the coincidence which alerts us to the phenomenon. Our awareness may be called to the matter through the patterns of symbolic connection being displayed around us. As a symbolic event, we recognise a significant moment is being enacted and we might grasp its meaning in that moment, or our understanding of it can develop through reflection and revisiting it and, as Maggie Hyde suggests, we may gain greater understanding of it over time.[3]

During the course of his lifetime's work exploring the world of the psyche and the nature of the unconscious Jung encountered many synchronicities in his own life and observed and recorded many arising for his clients. Perhaps one of his best-known examples is that of the appearance of the golden scarab. Jung was with a patient who dreamt the night before of being given an expensive piece of jewellery in the form of a golden scarab. As she told him the dream Jung heard a tapping at the window which he opened to reveal a large golden green scarabaeid beetle which was attempting uncharacteristically to get into the dark room. He tells how he caught the beetle and gave it to his client, and how subsequently this powerful experience broke through the client's rigid rational defences and enabled the therapeutic process to begin.[4] He observed that synchronicities seemed to arise at times of significant transformation or change for individuals and coincided with periods of inner development and transition.[5] Indeed Jung considered that the synchronous event itself seemed to contribute to transformation, as if the revealed awareness of the connection between inner and outer reality contributes to the process of personal integration for the participant and leads to an awakening of a wider sense of meaning in life.[6]

Jung observed that at each synchronous experience the pattern being constellated seemed to connect with an archetype. In recognising the symbolic dimension of the phenomenon he realised that archetypes are fundamental to synchronicity.[7] Informed by Jung's work, which built on philosophical perspectives stretching back to Plato's Ideas, archetypes have come to be regarded as the fundamental and timeless patterns which structure life and give it meaning. These innate symbolic images, which as perennial forms have a numinous and mythic quality, are embedded in the depth of the psyche and their symbolic patterning extends throughout the personal and collective dimensions of existence. It is these symbolic forms which are constellated in a synchronous event and evoke their archetypal meaning which is recognisable in the outer manifestation and in the inner psychological awareness. In the scarab synchronicity, the beetle is associated with the Egyptian Sun god, who in his myth is transformed into a scarab as he travels through the underworld and then re-emerges at dawn as the god to be carried up into the sky on his barque. The scarab then is an archetypal symbol of death and rebirth, and his appearance in the dream and the therapy room illuminated the process of renewal underway for the client.

From his first description of meaningful coincidence in 1928, Jung spent several decades investigating this phenomenon seeking to explain the underlying principle at work, such that by the early 1950s he set about articulating a wider theory of synchronicity. Drawing ideas from many wisdom traditions which reflected the concept of the unified above and below, encompassing the Chinese Tao, the Renaissance law of correspondences and the *Unus Mundus* of the alchemists, he was seeking a theory to explain these occurrences through which the archetypes manifest objectively in external events and have an inner corollary in psychic awareness.

He was recognising that in seeing the archetypal pattern expressed both within and without, he could not view the archetype as a pattern held only within the inner psychic dimension but rather one which extends throughout psyche and matter. The synchronicity makes a connection between inner life and outer world as it shows itself in both domains and in doing so it transcends the separation between the two. In this bilateral expression, it integrates the modern Cartesian division of inner-outer, subject-object, mind-matter, and unites the individual with the world. As Rick Tarnas explains, whilst in his early career Jung wrote about archetypes as inner psychic forms, in his work with synchronicity he was now coming to view archetypes as existing beyond the psyche and creating a bridge between psyche and matter. In this he was approaching the ancient idea of the *Anima Mundi*, the Soul of the World, where psyche and matter are not separate but part of a unified whole.[8] Reflecting on the process of working with synchronicity over time, as Tarnas describes, the body of Jung's work shows how the process might begin with vague or ambiguous perceptions of coincidence which might lead to more powerfully meaningful events such that a turning point might be reached for the individual engendering an awareness of the world as more connected, unified, whole. Then within this new worldview experiences of synchronicity might be incorporated into life as symbolic events which are sources of meaning and patterns to act on and navigate by.[9]

As astrologers it seems then that alongside learning the symbols and correspondences and technical components of the astrological chart, we are also beginning to alter our worldview and inhabit the world differently. For many of us the rational scientific framework we have been inducted into from an early age begins to shift as we enter the world of astrology and begin to study, meet with fellow astrologers, and engage with the world through these new series of symbols and correspondences. We begin to notice synchronicities around us informed by our new symbolic knowledge and after a while this new astrological way of viewing the world becomes self-reinforcing. And as we perceive interconnections between events that are not causal or mechanistic we start to live in a more symbolic world.

A similar process has been studied anthropologically, not amongst astrologers but amongst magicians. An American academic, Tanya Luhrmann, began studying the British magical community in the late 1980s. She identified how, as people began coming to groups and reading and studying magic they began to shift their perceptions about the world from the causal scientific view to a world that became more symbolic, less explicable by cause and effect, more informed by correspondences and symbolic connections and synchronicities. She identified this phenomenon as 'interpretive drift', where people began to interpret their world differently in line with a more symbolic view that fitted their new way of looking at the world that is connected by correspondences and imbued with supernatural and divine powers.[10] This same process I would suggest is what happens when we enter the sphere of astrology. Our worldview changes and we slowly adapt to a new perspective where we perceive and make sense of our world in terms of astrologically-informed symbolic correspondences and patterns, and in doing so we begin to recognise in the moment the significance of synchronicities or symbolic patterns or become more sensitive to receiving feedback from the world as omens or auguries. Luhrmann describes several occasions where she became aware of this happening to her. On one occasion she was travelling on a train back from a meeting when she experienced a significant moment of heightened awareness which she says she might have later ignored or explained away were it not for the fact that she found that her watch had stopped synchronistically at the very same moment.

## COSMOLOGY

A dimension of this new landscape that I was now being called to explore was my orientation to the world. Standing on the earth physically and looking out at the sky and the moon, or placing myself imaginally at the centre of an astrological chart and paying attention to the passage of the planets moving across the heavens against the backdrop of stars, I was consciously becoming earth-centred in my view of the cosmos. Indeed, one of the transitions we make as we come into astrology is a shift away from the heliocentric worldview of our modern Western scientific culture. This prevailing sun-centred paradigm has been informed by modern astronomy which recognises that our solar system revolves around our central star. Supported by telescopic images of the cosmos taken from beyond the bounds of the earth we have reimagined our solar system centred on the sun and then viewed on a trajectory out beyond Pluto in a perspective which dislocates us into a revolving orbit between Venus and Mars. And subsequently our central sun has been imagined as just one of innumerable, countless numbers of stars. Yet, as I began to work with charts and follow the planets across the sky and through the zodiac, from viewing the world from the dominant heliocentric model, I was taking steps into inhabiting a geocentric world.

This earth-centred view of the cosmos has been the perspective of humanity for millennia. It stretches back into the preceding ages before the relatively recent 17th century revolution in worldview heralded in by the Copernican revolution and the Scientific Enlightenment which has detached us from our anchorage at the centre of our cosmos and from our experience of the world as living and ensouled. Although Hermeticism and Neoplatonism had influenced the development of experimental science, the emerging scientific view deployed methods based on observation, experimentation and obtaining concrete data, and through adopting this approach increasingly the world has come to be understood through causal relationships and mechanised processes alone.[11] As the philosopher Mary Midgley has examined, this now-dominant rational mechanistic paradigm is based upon an objective empirical approach to the world,[12] and within such a paradigm the practices which enable non-rational means of understanding and of relating to a sacred cosmos which is experienced as alive and meaningful have been culturally displaced.[13] The scientific view, operating through rationality, objectivity and cause and effect, values that which is material, tangible and rational, whilst in this framework psyche and spirit can no longer be explained. This leaves little room for imagination or the non-rational, and seen through this lens the world has become devoid of soul and living agency as these spiritual and imaginal elements have been rejected or abandoned. This worldview, which has come to dominate our modern life experience, is built upon this split between the material and spiritual dimensions of life, and consequently the worldview which supports a magical, symbolic and spiritual relationship with the world has been marginalised in our current era.

Standing in contrast to the modern scientific outlook, this ancient geocentric view of the cosmos that I was now beginning to step into and inhabit has informed cosmological perspectives which stretch back to the ancient world. Developed in Neoplatonism and subsequently informing Medieval and Renaissance philosophy, the neoplatonic map is imagined showing three layers or levels of reality and places us on the earth at the centre of our world where we are surrounded by the planetary spheres and the stars. These realms are laid out in concentric rings around each other and might each be perceived as deeper levels of reality where the outer encompasses and permeates the inner layers. The celestial realm of the fixed stars is associated with the spiritual world around which the divine encompasses and circumscribes the cosmos. Lying beneath this layer

## THE INITIAL AWAKENING

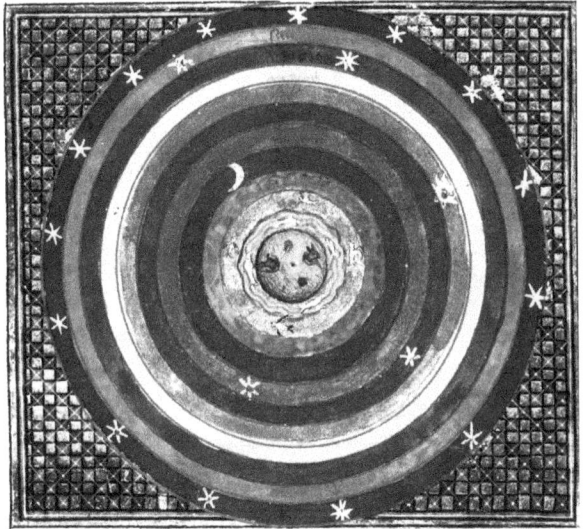

The Pre-Modern Cosmos

is the planetary realm associated with psyche or soul. Here we find the seven spheres of the traditional planets bounded by Saturn who with his rings marks the edge of the visible planetary world, and lying successively beneath him the spheres of the planets down to Mercury and closest to earth, the moon. And at the heart of the cosmological image, beneath the moon, in the sub-lunar world is the material realm. This is the sphere of earth and the place of the four elements and this realm too is perceived as alive and imbued with soul.[14]

As a cosmology which supports the astrological perspective, we can see how this image informs our astrological chart. The three realms of the divine, the psyche and the physical world are all interconnected by symbolic correspondences in the great web of connection of life which is viewed as spanning the divine realms through humanity to the animals, plants and all the myriad material expressions of life on earth. It is this framework that astrologers are encountering when learning planetary correspondences in order to perceive planetary patterns and thereby find meaning as symbolic links are recognised running across the planetary spheres and through corresponding levels of reality. The astrologer, adapting to a geocentric worldview which is linked by correspondences and their revealed patterns of meaning, discovers entry to a world which appears alive, responsive and symbolically meaningful. No longer a detached, inert background for life the cosmos becomes imbued with agency, and no longer simply an observer of life, the astrologer becomes a participator in this living reality.

## PARTICIPATION

The mode of engaging with and experiencing the world with its moments of connection and meaning has been described by anthropologists as participation. This anthropological term derives from examining cultures which are animistic, where the world is imbued with life, where the land is perceived as awake and can be communicated with directly and where there is no separation between the person and the landscape they live in or between the human and the divine. This concept of participation was first proposed by the French anthropologist Lucien Lévy-Bruhl in the early 20th century who described it as an approach or way of experiencing the world that is non-rational and based upon feeling and reflection rather than logic and reason. It is characterised by a fusing together of the experience between subject and object which generates a sense of mystical unity.

Developing these ideas the anthropologist Stanley Tambiah subsequently suggested that participation, with its sensory and feeling orientation to the world, is polarised with causality which approaches the world through rationality and cognition. The causal mode of perception embraces rules, requires data and uses the language of analytical and logical reasoning, hence it is the orientation of a scientific outlook. In contrast, participation emphasises communication through the senses and relationship which is grounded in place and as such it relates to magical, artistic and religious experience, and it is this mode which enables a relationship to take place between the individual and the spiritual dimension of life. Significantly, Tambiah considered that causality and participation are not separate ways of being in the world but are co-existent where these two ways of engaging with reality are both available to an individual such that we might be able to experience life both through a causal lens and also through a participatory lens and thus be able to inhabit both worlds. As historian Wouter Hanegraaff shows however, whilst both modes may be co-existent natural abilities of

## THE INITIAL AWAKENING

the mind, the contemporary cultural context informs our relationship to these two orientations. Whilst rationality comes easily to us in our modern Western culture, the participative mode lacks cultural acceptance and it is thus much harder for us to access these more participative states of mind. Yet in shifting between these two modes of perception we have the ability to change our relationship with the world from detached observer to mutual participator, and in altering our perception we may be able to experience participation with the world outside ourselves where the subject-object, inner-outer, self-world split is temporarily bridged and the world comes alive with its moments of connection, meaning, symbolic awareness and synchronicity. In so doing we may be stepping beyond the rational cosmos of the modern era to re-enter a sacred, living world.[15]

Astrology in its relationship with the symbolic world calls us to travel beyond the rational and objective dimensions of our current worldview. The journey we each take with astrology, with its moments of heightened awareness, synchronicities, symbolic patterns and meaningful connections made through symbols and correspondences, opens up a new perspective on the world and in response to this our world changes. This new way of relating to life brings about a significant personal reorientation such that, guided by astrology, we journey into a new way of being in the world that is enlivened, enriched and made meaningful through astrological patterns of meaning. We may little imagine that the journey we start out on when we take our first class or open our first astrology book may lead into a new relationship with the cosmos, yet as many astrologers who have travelled this path attest to, the astrological journey has the potential to bring about a rich sense of meaning in the cosmos, engender deep inner change and offer nothing less than a new relationship with life itself.

### NOTES

1. A number of interviews were carried out with fellow astrologers in the summer of 2014 from which this material is drawn.

2. Carl G. Jung, Ed, *Man and His Symbols* (London: Picador, 1978) [hereafter *Man and His Symbols*], p.226.

3. See Maggie Hyde, *Jung and Astrology* (London: The Aquarian Press, 1992), pp.123-125 for discussion on finding meaning in synchronicity.

4. Carl G. Jung, *Synchronicity: An Acausal Connecting Principle* (London: Routledge and Kegan Paul, 1955) [hereafter *Synchronicity*], p.31.

5. *Man and His Symbols*, p.227.

6. See Richard Tarnas, *Cosmos and Psyche, Intimations of a New World View* (New York: Viking, 2006) [hereafter *Cosmos and Psyche*], pp.50-60 for discussion on Jung and synchronicity.

7. *Synchronicity*, p.34.

8. *Cosmos and Psyche*, p.57.

9. *Cosmos and Psyche*, p.55.

10. Tanya Luhrmann, *Persuasion of the Witch's Craft: Ritual Magic in Contemporary England* (Oxford: Blackwell, 1989), p.307.

11. Charles Webster, *From Paracelsus to Newton, Magic and the Making of Modern Science* (Cambridge: Cambridge University Press, 1982).

12. Mary Midgley, *Science as Salvation* (London and New York: Routledge, 1992).

13. See Graham Harvey, *Animism: Respecting the Living World* (London: Hunt & Co, 2005) for a discussion of this process.

14. For a recent description of this cosmological model see Angela Voss, 'Astrology as Divine Revelation: Some thoughts on Ibn Arabi's Understanding of Imagination', *The Astrological Journal*, Vol. 56, No. 6, Nov/Dec 2014, p.15.

15. For further discussion on participation see Stanley Tambiah, *Magic, Science, Religion and the Scope of Rationality* (Cambridge: Cambridge University Press, 1990), pp. 84-110. The concept was originally proposed in Lucien Lévy-Bruhl, *How Natives Think* (Princeton: Princeton University Press 1985 [1910]). See also Wouter J. Hanegraaff, '*How Magic Survived the Disenchantment of the World*', Religion, Vol. 33, (2003), pp. 375-378.

Chapter Two
# THE ART OF INTERPRETATION
## CAROLE TAYLOR

Interpretation is the very essence of the astrologer's art. The symbols of the horoscope are full of meaning, waiting to tell their story – they can reveal character and circumstance, a life lived, the potential for skills yet to be developed and events yet to come, the whole shape of a person's life. Technical knowledge is one thing (and all astrologers, no matter how esoteric or psychological their leanings, need some kind of technical foundation from which to work), but our art rests on an ability to draw meaning from a birth chart, to see reflected in it the complexities of a human personality, embedded in its cultural, social and familial context. Even if we take the view that the birth chart does not describe external reality but only our perception of it, there is still the idea that somewhere in the chart we will find descriptors for all the experiences that person will ever have, along with everything they might have yearned for but never achieved. Our approach to interpretation must attempt to encompass this and seek to reflect something of life's pain, joy, paradoxes and contradictions.

Astrology offers a bewildering array of concepts for us to play with – branches of study, techniques, house systems (15 of them and counting...), celestial bodies; whatever it is, astrology will usually give you an overwhelming amount of choice. The astrologer Bernard Eccles, in a talk at the Faculty's Summer School one year, showed a chart in which he had included all the possible bodies and types of aspect offered by his astrological software – it was so densely packed with overlapping glyphs and lines, it was impossible to distinguish anything at all. We can keep adding chart factors and new techniques into the mix, fearful that the latest asteroid or Trans-Neptunian Object might offer the one vital piece of information that finally decodes the client's chart, but there comes a point where adding more stuff in just begins to produce 'white noise', a distraction from going deeper into the individual symbols. Each chart factor offers a wealth of meaning and can only begin to yield that meaning if we take the time to listen. From this point of view, less is often more – or at least, to me it seems a better strategy to get to know the basic things very well rather than spread oneself liberally over the whole solar system; a dish with just a few ingredients usually tastes better than one which contains everything you could find in the cupboards.

Every student of astrology begins with keywords. I remember making endless lists of them in the early years – planets, signs and houses, aspects and aspect patterns, lists on neat cards and scraps of paper, larger sheets for mind maps, lost for hours in the Mercurial bliss of moving words and phrases around in endless combinations. Venus – love, relationships, style, values, aesthetics, artistry, joy, seduction; Saturn – duty, weight, gravity, lead, black, boundaries, stop, no; then Venus-Saturn – relationships with rules, enjoys dressing in black; you get the picture. It was a whole new world. I knew very little about astrology before I stumbled across the Faculty in 1995; I booked for the Foundation class because I had discovered Pythagoras and Kepler and was on a mission to learn more about musical harmonics and sacred number, and astrology seemed like an interesting place to start. But like the Tarot Fool about to step off the cliff, I was unaware of the transformational effect astrology would have on me – Pluto was making a square aspect by transit to my natal 3rd house Uranus, and I remember that first astrology class in September 1995 down to the smallest detail because it was the day the whole world suddenly came alive; from that day on every colour was just that bit brighter, every experience just that bit more meaningful, both an awakening and a homecoming.

Planets are wonderful enough just by themselves, but then – oh joy! – there are 12 zodiac signs and 12 houses too. It was a whole new vocabulary, indeed a whole new language. I played continually with it and then slowly the keywords started to attach themselves to real people. I took a notebook with me everywhere to write down ideas, observing people on buses or in cafés, trying to guess their Ascendant from the look of them or their Moon sign from physical gestures or the way they were drinking their coffee – Virgo's careful use of the napkin, Aries looking in horror at the length of the queue. If Mars means 'how we fight' and Scorpio is associated with death and rebirth, then Mars in Scorpio signifies someone who takes no prisoners and is prepared to fight to the death rather than concede to the enemy – and then, of course, there came the revelatory moment when I actually met someone with Mars in Scorpio, sensed the nuclear warhead ready and primed, and knew instinctively that I would not want to lock horns with him.

And from keywords can come great things – even a word can become a symbol and can point, like Hermes at the crossroads, to a multiplicity of meanings. I realised that people 'fight' in all sorts of different ways, that for each person it represents the defence of personal territory, particularly of those things into which we pour our energy and which therefore become invested with our life force, of which Mars is a potent image. A whole new type of vocabulary arose to add to my burgeoning Martian keyword cards and mind maps – mode of attack, defensive position, assault weapon, task force, close combat, zone of fire, active duty. I trawled websites for things like military terminology to add flavour – Mars in Sagittarius as 'here come the cavalry' or 'the charge of the Light Brigade', Mars in Capricorn as 'tactical manoeuvres', Mars in Scorpio as 'scorched earth policy'. And that's only one dimension of Mars within the chart, of course – as with any symbol we can never reach the end in our understanding of a planet and can only continue to explore the possibilities.

This was my way in, at least – with three planets and the Ascendant in Gemini and a crowded 3rd house, words hold tremendous power for me; I have always been fascinated by etymology and delighted by wordplay, and I felt the need to translate the beautiful symbols of astrology into words and phrases that would perfectly distil their essence, bringing them closer to me through the Hermetic device of language. I read as much as I could, and of course still do, although nowadays it's not so much astrology textbooks which I feel fed by, but myth, literature and poetry – anything where I might find an astrological symbol staring back at me from the page. For others of a less Mercurial nature, there will doubtless be other approaches – putting together scrapbooks of images, collecting objects, creating artworks, and so on. Each person's journey through astrology is unique and the process of learning the subject reflects our own chart and the route of personal development which flows from it. For me, the act of learning and practising astrology has been paralleled by the process

*Hermes polytropos*

of developing linguistic and verbal skills, and I believe both processes have been equally crucial and central to my life story.

Compiled with thoughtfulness and attention, I believe that the use of keywords and key phrases, such as the ones students are often encouraged to work with in the note-taking process, can be an effective doorway into a chart, capturing the core essence of the symbols – from there we can expand each concept into a range of different interpretations which all retain that core essence. As Liz Greene has pointed out, how we see life is how we read charts[1], so we will always interpret symbols from our own point of view, but key phrases can be a useful and effective part of the ritual of working on a chart, at any stage of the game but particularly in the early years of building confidence and fluency – they conjure mental images which (if we are careful) offer an 'archetypal' understanding, so that we remain open to the range of possibilities rather than calcifying the information into a personal fantasy about the chart's owner.

Of course, it's the 'if we are careful' part of things which counts here – there is always the danger that we try to make a chart fit with our own views of what it must be like. Many times I've heard astrologers

## THE ART OF INTERPRETATION

describing Moon-Saturn definitively as a 'lack of mothering', as if it were inevitable that anyone with this placement must have suffered from an absence of maternal affection. In the Homeric Hymn to Hermes, the poet describes Hermes as *polytropos* – literally 'turning many ways'; this is perhaps the frame of mind we need with keywords (well, with any interpretation), as a distillation of an idea which is as neutral as we can make it, and which acts as the starting point for exploration with the client. The 'fight to the death' of Mars in Scorpio, for instance, can play itself out on all sorts of different levels that would require us to ponder the nature of what is being fought for and the purpose of the 'rebirth' which might follow the 'death' – we need to bring attention and thought to the deeper implications so that it can be the starting point for further dialogue, fleshed out by the client's own experience.

### MYTHS AND STORIES

Myths and fairy tales, including their modern counterparts in film and literature, further amplify our understanding of astrological symbols, helping us to move from simple keyword interpretations to a view of the chart as a collection of narratives drawn from archetypal components (Venus-Pluto as the story of Inanna in the underworld, Uranus-Saturn as the story of the castration of the sky god by his son Kronos, and so on), before we set them within the unique circumstances of the individual's life. Being a lover of myth, I have learnt a great deal from it, writers such as Joseph Campbell, Karl Kerényi, Jean Shinoda Bolen and Jules Cashford taking up large amounts of shelf space in my house. Their work has been hugely influential for me, almost more so than astrological texts (the exceptions here being astrologers such as Liz Greene, Darby Costello, Melanie Reinhart, Lynn Bell, Brian Clark and Clare Martin, whose work is suffused with an understanding of myth and therefore offers the reader rich possibilities for further exploration and insight).

But all this only takes us so far. We learn astrology best by seeing it in action in people's lives – this is where it begins to lift off the page, through careful observation and listening, the respectful interchange with clients in chart readings, and through watching our own charts unfold over time. I also believe we need to make a relationship to the symbols, recognising that they are archetypal or quintessential energies which live and breathe in the world around us. It is this, along with the personal changes described in the preceding chapter, which move us from simple metaphoric translation of the chart to a deeper understanding, and it is these ideas that I want to turn to.

## FLEXING THE IMAGINATION

Keywords have their limits – they are a primary stage or, later, a way of mentally storing complex ideas in linguistic form, a starting point for deeper contemplation. Imagination takes things further. The astrologer Geoffrey Cornelius, in an article in *The Astrological Journal* in 2014, made the comment that 'Behind each astrological interpretation is an act of imagination, since interpretation depends on the active manipulation of mental constructs, imagery and association, fitting them to the worldly situation before us'.[2] Imagination is vital in working with astrological symbols, since each chart is so complex and each symbol can have so many different meanings. Imagination is also vital in working with people. For instance, unless you have Saturn in Virgo in the 10th house yourself, you have to access a knowledge of it initially via the imagination – the keywords might say 'diligent attention to detail in one's career', but imagination can give us an image of what it might be like to inhabit the chart that contains this placement, from cradle to grave, with its continual demand for excellence and the quiet shouldering of responsibility, each achievement only serving to push the standard higher but offering the possibility of making one's mark in the world through solid professional accomplishments. And still further, imagination can allow us to glimpse possible patterns in the family history that also speak of Saturn's presence – the relationship to parental expectations and, further back, perhaps an ancestral thread concerned with the elevation of duty above other considerations and the sacrifices this might require. In particular, it takes imagination to feel what it might be like to walk a mile in that person's shoes, not to 'become' their Saturn inadvertently by telling them how they should feel or what they should do next, but allowing them to tell their own story.

So of course we must listen too – along with imagination, the ability to listen is one of the most important skills an astrologer can develop. The philosopher Epictetus said that we have two ears and one mouth so that we can listen twice as much as we speak, which might be hard for the astrologer who is nervous of not conveying the whole chart and all the forecasting to the client, nervous of not giving value for money if something is left out. But if we listen carefully, we hear the client speaking their own chart and the symbols move into another zone altogether. No two people with Saturn in Virgo in the 10th house will experience it in exactly the same way – the keywords we come up with in our preparation give us a foundation, an archetypal image from which to work, but (to borrow a phrase from Carl Rogers, the founder of person-centred counselling) the client is the expert on their own chart and will tell us more about it than any text book ever could.

The development of fluency with interpretation is therefore a complex thing, growing as our knowledge of the symbols expands, but flowering through the imagination and through careful listening and observation.

## MORE ABOUT IMAGINATION: ACTIVE IMAGINATION AND THE *MUNDUS IMAGINALIS*

In the article already cited, Geoffrey Cornelius, referencing the work of Henry Corbin, also makes the distinction between imagination as an act of metaphoric image-making and imagination as 'the mode of perception granted to the soul'. Further, he talks about Corbin's idea of the *mundus imaginalis*, an intermediate place between the material and divine worlds which is 'known symbolically, and is fully reflected in, or shadowed in, our ordinary material reality'. [3] Corbin created the term *mundus imaginalis*, the imaginal world, to describe this intermediate place – and Geoffrey Cornelius reminds us that imagination is 'the vital faculty by which this world is known'.[4]

The planets have been equated to the gods since ancient times, the zodiac signs represent a collection of larger-than-life celestial stories, the houses collectively give us nothing less than the totality of life's arenas of experience, and the aspects are based on Pythagorean ideas of sacred number reflecting, on one level, the very creation of the cosmos. It's big stuff. We will look further at the nature of symbols in a moment, but it seems clear to me that learning how to interpret a chart is not just a question of learning a set of metaphoric equations – Mars means this, Saturn means that – nor even of making those equations meaningful to a client. A revelation for me in my first year of study was seeing that the planets are the gods of antiquity, re-envisioned by Carl Jung as collective archetypes. We are entering 'sacred' territory with the chart, whether we take this in the sense of encounters with deities or cosmic forces, or in the secular sense of exploring deeper psychic content, conscious and unconscious, personal and collective.

In the time-honoured way within many spiritual traditions, imagination is our major organ for perception of, and connection to, the divine. We are talking here not just of 'imagination' in the sense of the ability to see images in the mind's eye, but also of 'active imagination' as described by Carl Jung and Henry Corbin, the kind of imagination which Geoffrey Cornelius is referring to above as a mode of spiritual reflection. Through this, we make a relationship to the chart as a sacred or other-worldly landscape. 'Active imagination' is therefore a deliberate process of engagement with a world that cannot be accessed using just our ordinary senses – we might think of it as a heightened state of awareness which allows the numinous symbols of the chart to come alive. Here we move towards a more personal experience of the symbols, offering the possibility of direct encounter with the 'deities' or psychic energy fields behind them.

## MEETING THE GODS

Astrologers sometimes call astrology a 'symbolic language' – perhaps more properly, it is a language made up of symbols, with its vocabulary of planets, signs, houses and aspects standing as descriptors for the interplay of feelings, motivations and actions which form the ground of a life. This can be deceptive, as though all we are doing in reading a chart is acting as a translator, untouched by the contents except for the bond of empathy which allows us to see things from the client's perspective. As Geoffrey Cornelius points out in the article already cited, much of the work done by astrologers, even those who work psychologically, proceeds on the basis that the astrologer is an objective observer, relaying information to clients about themselves.

But a symbol is indicative of a living energy and I think there is a turning point in our understanding when we feel it at work within ourselves and arising in the world around us, particularly when we see that the former usually coincides with the latter. Whether we believe the planets are 'divine entities' or simply archetypes within the unconscious is not the concern here – more that our understanding of them is taken to another level through direct encounter.

We can take as a starting point the words of Carl Jung in describing a symbol: '...a word or an image is symbolic when it implies something more than its obvious and immediate meaning. It has a wider "unconscious" aspect that is never defined or fully explained'.[5] What is implied here is that a symbol is not consciously contrived but acts as the potent image of a truth not immediately accessible to the conscious mind. Intellect does not reveal a symbol's deeper resonances because it seems to carry a numinous quality and evoke an emotional response. And since it defies concrete description or explanation, we must perhaps create a different kind of relationship to it, one which invites emotional interchange, a view which seems to accord with Joseph Campbell's definition of a symbol as 'an energy-evoking, and directing, agent'.[6]

Here I would like to refer to a method of interpreting symbolic material known as the 'four senses' hermeneutic, long used as a model in the interpretation of religious scripture but which can also be applied to other symbolic content – indeed, it has been applied beautifully to astrology by Geoffrey Cornelius in his book *The Moment of Astrology*.[7]

The 'fourfold' method describes a sequence of experience in relation to a symbol or text, moving from literal translation to mystical participation or oneness with the symbol's essence. It is rooted in classical Greek analysis of the ancient poets (Homer in particular), but was taken up by Christian scholars and reached its height in the Medieval period, becoming the primary model for Biblical interpretation until Martin Luther. Used by Dante in The Divine Comedy, it was adopted in the Renaissance as a way of approaching art as a container for divine truth, but in essence it can be applied to any symbolic form – glyphic, poetic, textual or artistic.

The four levels are the literal, the allegorical or typological, the moral or tropological, and the anagogical or mystical. For instance, in reading the Bible, it is possible to take any portion of the text literally, at face value, as a report of historic events or facts. The purpose of the allegorical level is to find a metaphor for the information in question – in Biblical interpretation it describes the device of connecting Old and New Testament stories so that the events of Christ's life are shown to be a fulfilment of Old Testament events; so we move to the next level of understanding by looking beyond literal facts to a metaphoric parallel.

At the moral level we encounter the 'moral of the story' – we are no longer a casual observer making intellectual comparisons, but recognise that the text or symbol is speaking directly to our situation. This third level is also described as tropological – literally our perception turns, like the watcher of a play when he realises that his own life is being described by the drama unfolding on the stage. Finally, we move to the anagogical or mystical level where we enter the heart of the mystery. In Biblical exegesis, it describes the detection within scripture of allusions to heaven and the afterlife; in our engagement with a planetary symbol, this level suggests achieving a 'felt sense' of the symbol's essence, such that the separation between symbol and observer falls away.

We can apply the model to any astrological symbol – in honour of my own presiding deity, I will choose Mercury for the purpose and first describe the process in theory before offering an example from my own experience which might serve to illustrate it in practice.

The glyph for astrological Mercury is constructed out of the three basic symbols which form the glyphs for all seven classical planets – the circle (symbolising eternal spirit) the semi-circle (soul) and the cross (the material world). We have, therefore, a composite symbol suggesting a confluence of the material, intermediary and divine, consistent (in the astrological view) with the character of Roman mythological Mercury, and his Greek and Egyptian counterparts (Hermes and Thoth), who functioned as messenger and scribe, the only deity with free passage between heaven, earth and underworld.

The literal level of this symbol's interpretation might call to mind the planet's astronomical properties. It has a speedy orbit and its angular distance from the sun is never more than 28° as seen from earth, making it elusive. It also has an elliptical and eccentric orbit, like a 'demented bee', in the phrase of Bernard Eccles.

The mythic image of Mercury expands our understanding at the allegorical level – in the classical myths, he bears the role of psychopomp or conductor of souls to the underworld, as well as inventor, thief, trickster, liar, storyteller and conveyor of messages. Often depicted in the myths as a youth, Mercury is the image of the 'puer' or eternal child, which might be interpreted as qualities of androgyny, youthful energy, versatility and adaptability, but also reluctance to settle or commit. Or we might consider the alchemical image of Mercurius who unites the King and Queen in the process of the alchemical work, showing Mercury as a symbol indicating the union of opposites.

As Geoffrey Cornelius points out in *The Moment of Astrology*, much of our work can be located at the allegorical level. Whatever the psychological depth of the interpretation, the astrologer works mostly through the act of interpreting one thing (the symbol of Mercury) in terms of another (the 'connecting and communicating' function in the owner of the chart), making parallels between the archetypal image and the client's own character or experiences: '….this suggests a skill at …'; '…you may be inclined to enjoy…', and so on. Thus the vast potential of the symbol's meaning is given a boundary in the movement from the universal image of Mercury to the particular circumstances of the client's life.

At this point we have the possibility of moving into a more direct relationship with the symbol at the tropological level, an experience which has implications for the astrologer reading the chart. As Jung states, a symbol 'hints at something not yet known'[8], which implies the idea of entering uncharted territory or crossing a threshold. In reading a chart for a client, the astrologer moves beyond the role of objective interpreter and recognises their own participation in the symbol's manifestation – Mercury in the charts (of astrologer, client and of the moment) becomes highly charged and 'active', perhaps revealing itself through mercurial events in the client-astrologer relationship – given Mercury's reputation as trickster, for instance, we might not be surprised to find miscommunication of information, unexpected changes of plan or the phone ringing in the middle of the reading, whenever this planet is prominent in the astrology under examination, with the astrologer as co-creator of such situations. The astrologer's gaze turns towards the symbol as it appears in her own chart, recognising that Mercury in the client's chart is connected to Mercury in her own – they are not two different Mercuries, but two manifestations of the same eternal truth which transcends the temporal and spatial boundaries of both charts.

We might consider the final mystical level as an encounter with the 'deity' or archetypal essence which the astrological symbol for Mercury is meant to represent, a realisation that the astrological glyph represents an impulse of the 'Divine', however one conceives this. We come to understand the 'Idea' of Mercury (I use a capital 'I' in allusion to Plato's notion of Divine Ideas), the experience of which may feel like an initiation into a mystery.

## A PERSONAL STORY

This story involves the Faculty, whose natal chart is included here. As you will see, it contains a conjunction of the Sun, Moon and Uranus in the sign of Gemini. At the beginning of the millennium, with Pluto opposing these Gemini planets by transit, we had reached a point where we knew that a good deal of change was needed – the course material and exam system both needed modernisation, and nothing was in electronic format but had to be photocopied and posted out, requiring an expensive office and associated equipment.

Initially we discussed how we might slowly alter the existing material; perhaps we could aim to reduce our overheads as we gradually put everything onto CD. In the midst of our deliberations, we received a letter from the local council informing us that the building which housed our office was being compulsorily purchased and would be demolished 'to make way for new developments'. During the ensuing weeks our administrative centre was literally razed to the ground and we temporarily suspended our distance learning course.

We held a residential meeting to plan the way forward. When we arrived at the conference centre, the staff had helpfully put our name on the meeting room door – Faculty of Astrological Studies – except, they had mistyped the word 'Astrological' and had described us as Agricultural

# THE ART OF INTERPRETATION

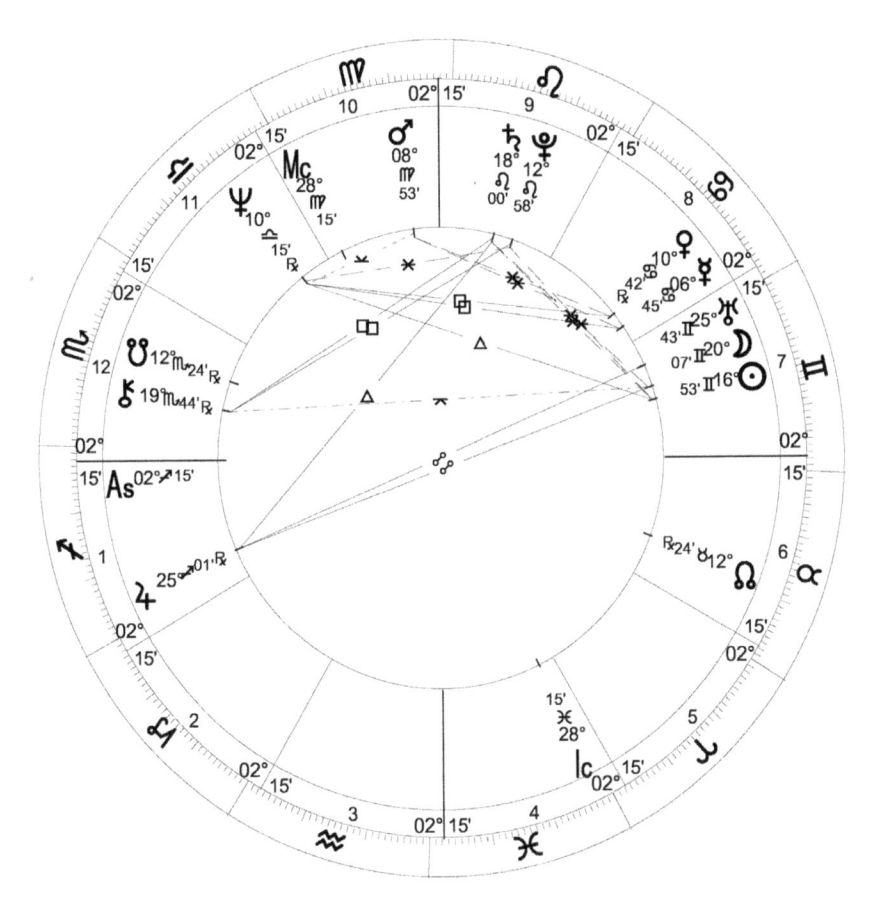

Faculty of Astrological Studies, 7 June 1948, 7.50pm, London, UK

Studies. In fact, they had also left the 'c' out of Faculty, so that the sign read 'Faulty Agricultural Studies'.

We might easily have dismissed this as a simple mistake. A literal reading of the sign would suggest merely a clerical error to which no meaning need be attached. Indeed, this was our initial response – a moment of levity at the beginning of what we knew would be a hard-working meeting.

But looking deeper, that sign was immensely significant and a perfect allegory for our situation. We were certainly 'faulty' – the old format was broken – and we acknowledged the need to address the very essence of what 'astrology' meant to us as an organisation, before we could recreate the course material and exams. This was a seminal moment in which the mental jolt engendered by the door sign seemed to reflect the radical alteration of perspective which was needed.

The horoscope for the meeting showed Gemini on the eastern horizon, at 19° 50', conjunct the Faculty's Sun-Moon-Uranus. Mercury, as ruler of Gemini, was therefore the chart's ruler, the 'presiding deity' of the moment. On that day he was making a tight conjunction to Uranus in Aquarius in the 9th house, a combination which neatly reflects both the unexpected error in the language of the door sign and the awakening to attention and change of perspective that resulted from it. Needless to say, we went on to completely rework our material, beginning with a blank piece of paper.

It would have been easy for me to leave things at this level of allegory, interpreted only in relation to the Faculty's chart, had I not been aware that the Mercury-Uranus conjunction was playing a significant role in my own horoscope – it conjoined my natal Saturn just as the Saturn of the moment conjoined my natal Mercury, ruler of my chart. My own nature, as you will have guessed by now, is highly Mercurial, prone to the 'perpetual motion' which the mythological image of Mercury/Hermes conveys – Saturn, by contrast, is a defining and containing energy, the antithesis of the Mercurial spirit. The astrology of the moment contained a very personal message, hand-delivered by Hermes – what had become 'set in stone' must be freed through a radical change of perspective (Mercury-Uranus on my Saturn); what had been in constant motion and dissipating its energies must be given greater form and definition (Saturn on my Mercury).

The 'trope' then was the moment of realisation that 'faulty agricultural studies' referred not only to the Faculty's situation but also to my own. Many aspects of my astrology had indeed become 'set in stone' and no longer provided room for growth – in other areas I felt lacking in knowledge and rigour. The result was that I went away and reviewed everything I had learnt, creating in the process a much richer understanding of astrology.

I believe it was this realisation that the symbol spoke also to me that allowed me to glimpse what might be thought of as the final level of interpretation – the 'mystical' level. I have no idea how to describe this, but it was apparent that the symbols of my own chart were capable of appearing in the outside world, as though called or invoked – it was a reminder that they were more than glyphs on a page, full of meaning but ultimately two-dimensional. I had strongly felt the presence of Hermes that day; in my mind's eye he had dashed into the corridor of the conference centre and switched the signs, laughing as he darted out of sight. I have come to see Mercury, and all the other planets, as a living reality and presence. My chart is no longer simply a map with symbols on it representing places I frequent or habit patterns I display – I am able to imagine past the glyph for Mercury to a place where he is a living force with whom I can dialogue, whether through the preparation for a chart reading, through ritual or invocation, or simply by feeling his spirit vital and alive within everything associated with him in the system of astrological correspondences. Through this experience, the world of ordinary reality – the literal form – has, for me, become suffused with the mysterious energy at the heart of the astrological planets; the mundane has been made sacred.

## KEEPING AT IT...

No one becomes an astrologer overnight. Within each person, the skills emerge in their own time, the never-completed process of learning paralleled by the never-completed process of self-development which astrology tends to galvanise. And since each of us possesses a unique chart, both of these processes will form a very personal journey, our interpretation skills developing and growing at each stage, such that the skills we come to offer our clients are also unique, reflecting our own particular gifts.

Interpretation can remain elusive – there will be times when the chart you are trying to read does not 'speak' to you and the experience can feel mechanical. At these times, we rely on our technical knowledge and our well-honed lists of keywords stored permanently in an easy-access memory bank. But there will also be times when the symbols truly come alive and these are the times that make astrology so magical and so fulfilling.

### NOTES

1. From a lecture at the Astrological Association Conference 2008 – see www.astro.com/astrology/in_lifeview_e.htm [accessed 31.10.2014].

2. Geoffrey Cornelius, 'Astrology, Imagination, Imaginal', in *The Astrological Journal*, Vol.56,

No. 1, Jan/Feb 2014 [hereafter *Astrology, Imagination, Imaginal*].

3. *Astrology, Imagination, Imaginal*.

4. *Astrology, Imagination, Imaginal*.

5. Carl G. Jung and Marie-Louise von Franz, eds, *Man and His Symbols* (London: Aldus Books, 1964), [hereafter *Man and His Symbols*], p.20.

6. Joseph Campbell, *Flight of the Wild Gander – Explorations in the Mythological Dimension* (California: New World Library, 2002), p.143.

7. Geoffrey Cornelius, *The Moment of Astrology* (Bournemouth: Wessex Astrologer, 2003). The astrologer and academic, Angela Voss, has also written quite extensively about this method of interpretation.

8. *Man and His Symbols*, p.55.

## Chapter Three
# NEGOTIATING THE FUTURE
## KIM FARLEY

### STARTING POINT

We are born into this world, we inhabit it and then we leave. The questions of where we came from and where we might go afterwards have always absorbed humanity, though it is what takes place during the stretch in between that counts for most of us.

As astrologers, we are used to thinking about our experience within a framework of meaning. Our cosmos, our solar system and our own particular birth chart call to us and if we listen we may discern what it wants – this slice of time that we somehow belong to, this moment which carries a blueprint for living. If we study it closely, perhaps we can visualise and construct a whole original person.

Or maybe instead, the chart is a kind of treasure map and the real search is an internal one. The map just serves as a useful reminder to keep looking, keep following the clues – *you are definitely in there somewhere.*

It has been observed that life can only be understood backwards, although it must be lived forwards. And also that, somehow, past, present and future are all a grand illusion anyway. I cannot grasp this and, inevitably, incomprehension forks two ways with me. The first way has a large hoarding which blocks the view and says 'Don't Think About It!' in primary colours with lots of pretty smiling faces and probably several web addresses. The second has a small sign which is harder to make out, but if I squint I think it reads 'This Way for the Interesting Stuff'. All the things we do not know – how wonderful, how magical they are. Trying to learn more is one reason to be alive, right there. If you happen to need a reason.

## TALKING TO CLIENTS

Clients come to astrologers to talk about their lives. At some point the talk moves from what is and what has been, towards what might be. So how do we cope with this part of the path? However well equipped with techniques we are, it is easy to lose our footing. The ground slopes away, the mist descends.

Of course, at the start, I was terrified by forecasting. A teenager in the late 1970's, my generation reverberated with Johnny Rotten's taunt: 'No Future'. And besides, I had no desire to examine some nebulous not-yet-happened while the very real here-and-now and been-and-gone were still baying for attention. And, more to the point, if I was so determined to swerve tightly away from whatever might be ahead, how could I possibly be trusted to steer anyone else?

As a novice practitioner, I almost buckled under my self-imposed burden. I felt the dead weight of responsibility and expectation as the hysterical voice in my head was wailing, 'These people demand to know what's going to happen to them and I have no idea! I can't do this!' Of course I wanted to do the best for those who came to see me; to offer them something useful, soulful, sensitive, illuminating. And alongside that I wanted to honour my craft and be worthy of serving it. This has not changed. Looking at it from my current perspective, the problem I struggled with then was mostly of my own making. Those who arrived at my door were usually far more relaxed about it all than I was. Nobody complained or denounced me; nobody seemed dissatisfied or disappointed at the end of their session. I was born under a Jupiter-Saturn conjunction in Capricorn which forms part of a T-square chart pattern and no doubt helps to hammer home a sense of duty and moral obligation, but in any case, I had created the perfect hook on which to writhe. Without sufficient confidence in myself, I found the confidence that clients invested in me created a kind of internal panic, desperate as I was not to betray their trust.

Sometimes it was so bad during preparation that I would more or less literally tear my hair and rend my garments at the prospect of delivering the requested forecasting – more than once I ended up on the carpet crying ten minutes before the buzz of my intercom. Even allowing for the dramatics of a tight natal Moon-Jupiter opposition, it was painful stuff. But since we do genuinely learn by going where we have to go, today I can be grateful to my early torturers for their crucial help. Yes, I had sat in my classes and read my books and done my work. I had put myself through the exams year by year; I knew the theory. And I spent hours in preparation. But it was not until I was required, over and over, to wrestle with the live reality of discussing the future that I developed any confidence in my own ability.

These days I find that the forecasting part of a consultation is where I feel most open to some kind of greater inspiration, free to fly. I no longer look down frozen in fear at the long drop, scared to take a step. As with so many endeavours, it was only by actually doing it that I really learned how.

## EARLY DAYS

Where did my journey through astrology begin? I try to think back and can only contact the sense that, like so many people, I was interested in the zodiac as a child. I must have looked at books and magazines enough to be aware of my own Sun sign and those of my close family and friends. As a six-year-old I was fixated on my own birthday to the extent that when my father asked me on the day before my mother celebrated hers, if I 'knew what was special about tomorrow?', I was able to squeeze out the answer that, 'yes, it was two months, two weeks and five days until my birthday'. Indeed, each autumn I would sit on the stairs in the early morning and ritually wait for the clock to crawl to five past seven, the time I had been born. Had my original appearance in the world taken place any later on in the day, I strongly doubt that this custom would have emerged.

It took another twenty or so years to pass before I found my way further into the subject. I can look back at the mid and late 1980s now and clearly trace the path that was forming, but at the time I was only aware of a series of disconnected steps. It was 1989 and the old world order was disintegrating, inside and out. I was twenty-eight. There had been a solar eclipse that summer which fell right on my 10th house Moon and I didn't know it then, but my whole direction had shifted and my path had been set. Nineteen years later the repeating eclipse on my Moon would again prefigure the hatching of a new parallel calling that fledged the following year and now perches alongside my astrology. Cycles of becoming, indeed.

I met my astrological vocation very literally in a Morley College creative writing class, when I found myself sitting next to Sue Tompkins. She was attending the first evening to see if she wanted to sign up to the course and in true Adult Education fashion we were all asked to talk to and then introduce our neighbour. Sue mentioned that she had just finished writing a non-fiction book (her now-classic *Aspects in Astrology*). I enquired and she allowed that it was on astrology, at which point my enthusiasm meter went off the scale and she probably wished I would just shut up, since she certainly did not want me to mention astrology to the group. In her classically dry way she then said if I was really that interested she would be teaching her own class the following week and so I scribbled down the details, already determined to attend. Sue never went to any further nights of that writing course and I, meanwhile, began my astrological education in earnest. That autumn, my Solar Return chart[1] contained an absolutely perfect Sun-Jupiter square.

Obsessed from the outset, I read everything I could and leapt upon anyone who showed the slightest inclination to talk astrology. I think I made my first attempt at a reading one week into term. Sometimes it is really useful to be completely oblivious to the vast stretches of your own ignorance.

The year and the decade turned. Directed Mars[2] (co-ruler of my Mercury, the planet associated with learning and ideas) was at that point square my Uranus (planet of liberation and awakening) and Uranus itself was now transiting square my Sun, leading to a huge sense of being woken up, though I was still unaware of all this. I recall Sue passing my desk one night and dropping in a casual observation on the latter, which I found both mysterious and thrilling. What did it represent? What was going to happen? If I stayed locked in a dark room would this strange and momentous thing still affect me? I felt a mixture of excitement and trepidation, not realising that I was already living out that Uranus transit on a daily basis – the heart of my life had been broken open and light was flooding in. The world was new and enchanting. At work as a receptionist, I sat at my desk drawing up and poring over charts until I was told to put away my papers and pens and behave.

I continued to hoover up books (thank you Lindsay River and Sally Gillespie, thank you Steven Arroyo, Charles Carter, thank you Howard Sasportas and Donna Cunningham and Tracey Marks and Christine Valentine and Liz Greene and most of all, thank you Sue) and to offer readings to anyone who wanted one. My calculation skills were getting there, but I was too impatient for all that, so in the beginning I leant heavily on a fellow Adult Education student who had become a friend. Joan was American. She had a tiny frame, a deep voice and a brilliantly dark world-view. More to the point, she owned a computer with astrological software on it. I would call and pester her and she would patiently input the data I gave her and read the placements to me down the phone line so that I could take up my felt pens and get going. It was 1990 and we had two topics of conversation which were never exhausted: astrology and Twin Peaks. Plus ça change.

I began to look for autobiographies to read alongside the charts of people who interested me and I remember the sense of revelation and delight at the way the life details and chart patterns illuminated and echoed each other. The first time I attempted a full interpretation I think I barely looked up for three days.

Attending my first ever Summer School, I was electrified, ecstatic. My progressed Sun[3] had reached the position of my natal Neptune by that point. I remember my birthday cards all had mermaids or water or fish on them that year. I was paying attention by then. Everything sang with meaning.

Over three terms of study in that Paddington classroom, Sue had been a constant source of inspiration, enlightenment and encouragement. Thanks to her, I was coaxed towards the Faculty Diploma. Uranus continued its lightning strikes to my Sun and directed Moon joined the fun by coming to conjunct my natal 11th house Uranus. Meanwhile directed Pluto came exactly to my Ascendant and my world changed. The first term of Diploma studies at that point involved ten blissful evenings of immersion in the symbolism of the planets, one planet a week and starting with Saturn. The day of that first class I had spent at a close friend's funeral up in Lancaster. I was dragging a heavy bag with me as I made my way into the wood-panelled room of the Royal Entomological society in Queen's Gate, Kensington, with its portraits of serious old men looming down from the walls. This, I believe, is called metanarrative.

## GETTING TO GRIPS

It was in that old-fashioned and elegant room the following year that I would first hear about forecasting. When I think back to my student years, it is that same room I picture, even though in time classes were moved to a modern light-filled space on the ground floor of the Urania Trust building in Caledonian Road. Back then, transits and progressions made up the core of forecasting studies and we had to hand-calculate all positions. There was nothing like the course material that exists today and we filled in any gaps ourselves. Education, as they say, is not a passive process. I cannot remember being told anything much about directions, nor even Solar Return charts. Different techniques were referenced, but not elucidated. I flung myself into everything from tertiary progressions to converse transits and tried to test it all out. Of course, it has been said that any technique works the first time you use it.

My own practice essentially concentrated almost entirely on transits for a long while. I felt that I knew where I was with the planets, just about, and so transits seemed to represent a firm handle for which to reach. Progressions seemed opaque and insubstantial to me, while directions and Solar Returns (both of which I value highly these days) were barely a twinkle in my eye.

Anyone who has come to investigate and stayed to revel in this amazing discipline will be familiar with the fact that most non-astrologers think – if they think anything – that we are some species of fortune teller. My partner's relatives imagine I work at the end of the pier and they are not alone – the notion that astrology is synonymous with prediction is encountered everywhere. In those early beginner classes with Sue, the headmaster would walk in to collect the overhead projector and always *always* say, 'but of course you knew I was coming in didn't you?' Quite apart from the fact that his appearance and his idea of humour were predictable, it underlined the popular misconception that star language is only ever concerned with what is yet to come.

Every consultant astrologer is bound to grapple at some point with the question of what it is they believe about the future. We naturally tend to incorporate our own ideas and attitudes into our forecasting, so we do at least need to be clear what these are. There is a world of difference between telling people 'this will happen', 'this might happen' and 'this seems

*Fortuna* (Hans Sebald Beham, 1541)

to be one of the many possibilities open to you', and indeed those very statements are themselves oriented towards describing events rather than exploring processes. What are we aiming to do? This is the first and most crucial question. It seems reasonable enough to suggest that, just as the birth chart outlines a combination of character and potential and needs context and dialogue to bring it to life, so might our efforts to forecast.

What is your own position? Do you see events as being detached from participants? Is there somehow a set framework into and through which we all simply wander, with no option to change what transpires? Are we, in other words, merely (sleep)walking towards the inevitable, any actions taken being nothing more than parts of an overall fate? What is fate? What is free will? The latter has been described as doing gladly whatever has been ordained, which clearly suggests we have very limited scope, other than to cheer up a bit. What do you believe? Are we like the servant in the fable of meeting death in Samarra, unconsciously travelling towards his fate when he thought he was acting to avoid it?[4] What is your own view on our collaboration with the future?

Much of our natal work as modern astrologers seems to issue from a strong sense that the inner and outer reflect each other, so why should forecasting differ in this respect? Is character, indeed, fate?

If, as consultant astrologers, we consider the pattern to be irrevocably set, then we are taking on a grave responsibility towards our clients, one with a power dynamic that I would personally find troubling. Of course, my attitude here is a function of my own cultural norms as well as my values and beliefs. In India and the Far East, for example, it is quite commonplace to expect explicit predictions from your astrologer. The issue remains – how do we read and interpret what we see and then how do we translate that?

## FINDING THE WORDS

Let's look at an example. Take, for instance, an imaginary male client whose forecasting points in various ways towards issues connected to partnership. It's perfectly possible that before the consultation we know nothing about whether he is already in a relationship or even if he dates women rather than men. Making a pronouncement such as 'you will meet your future wife in July' is of no use and would be ludicrous to a man who is with a long-term boyfriend. On the other hand, opening up a conversation about longing, discussing the possibility of experiencing feelings of strong attraction and talking about being porous to desire could be both relevant and very helpful.

I would always hope that any forecasting I offer is as meaningful and as truthful as I can make it, but I am clear that I do not know what is going to take place. One person may use their feelings of wanting something more – their will to share and delight in this world – by creating art or forging friendship or community. Another may initiate an affair. The phrase 'I didn't plan for this to happen' is so often employed in the face of turbulent circumstances. If we had been to see an astrologer and talked in depth through the potential of the time ahead, perhaps our own agency – and indeed sense of having had a choice in the first place – would be a little clearer. Perhaps.

As with all consultation work, dialogue and listening are the essential beginning. The natal chart is the primary framework and context for our forecasting, but even with all the techniques and tools in the world, so much hinges on how we put over the information we have distilled from the symbolism.

In my own practice, I try to remain open to many possibilities, since only hindsight is 20/20. Rather than attempting to tell someone what will happen or, much less, what action they should take, I try to imaginatively explore the potential that the time ahead offers them – to outline a variety of choices or scenarios connected to the principles at play. As with any journey, where one might end up is intimately connected to where one begins.

When you learn a language, the present tense tends to be your introduction. As you progress you may learn the past tense, and in time, the future. An examination of English grammar reveals that there are several ways of talking about time yet to come and astrology is no different. But we are of course aiming to employ language specific to an individual, in terms which are both relevant and meaningful.

Those of us engaged in speaking, translating and interpreting star language, sooner or later discover that we also have various ways to think about and express our ideas on future time. Every craft has its particular techniques and tools with which to work. But the real issue is how we deliver that information. How do we take the fact that Pluto will conjunct someone's Moon next year and use it to offer them a truthful, useful, sensitive account of the potential contained therein? This is the work.

I think back to the clients of my true apprenticeship and remember their questions: 'What will happen with my job?', 'Will I move house?', 'Will I get pregnant?', 'Will I meet my birth father?' My answer always began with 'I don't know what's going to happen to you' followed by 'but it seems to me that this time reflects something about....' as I tried to describe the sketched outlines of a shifting picture which only they could ink and colour in. Of course, I would have spent plenty of time preparing before the consultation, using different ways of thinking about the symbolism and trying to stretch and flex my imagination to seek out the creative, meaningful and practical potential of the rich symbols. Each time a person returned to me after a reading, usually many, many months, if not years, later and told me, 'It happened exactly as you said' I would think 'but I never said anything exact!' and feel a strange mixture of confusion, satisfaction and relief.

It took me a long time to trust myself as an astrologer. What I learnt early on, however, is that I could always trust the astrology itself. I could trust the planets and the framework of the natal chart through which they moved. I could trust that when Neptune crossed the client's Capricorn Ascendant and Sun, it would represent a time when her identity was changing (and yes, she did meet her birth father) or that when Jupiter stationed on another client's 4th house ruler (signifying expansion to home), it would reflect an increased sense of space and connection (and yes, she did move house). Each time I heard about the symbolism playing out in people's lives in a way that entirely made sense, I gained a little more confidence in my ability to discuss the outlines as I understood them.

It's almost inevitable that people seek astrological guidance when their lives are unclear or uncomfortable in some way. I do not recall a client ever saying to me 'I want a reading because things are just going so well and I'm really happy right now'. Though some consultations come about due to people simply being interested in and open to what astrology has to say about their lives, it is still noteworthy that they chose this moment to engage in the dialogue. Talking over your chart can be incredibly validating and give a sense of truly inhabiting your history and experience. It can return a feeling of connection and agency to a situation where previously one might have felt powerless or alienated. Above all, an astrological perspective can inspire, encourage and illuminate, injecting something vital back into our relationship with our own existence. This is in fact one of the core reasons I love working with clients – the astrology gives me a framework and a language in which to name and to celebrate their potential to do the things that some deeper part of them has already identified. It is a privilege to be able to translate this language into meaningful, practical affirmation and to help them glimpse the wealth of possibilities their life contains. There is no better job, it seems to me.

## NEGOTIATING THE FUTURE

### BEING REAL

And at this point you might well be thinking 'hang on a minute, that all sounds too good to be true – what about all the ordinary pain and suffering, the loss and disappointment, the grief and destruction and misery that exists?' Ah yes. That. Well, what I've found is that if you are with someone who is in the middle of it, there is a huge relief in the acknowledgement. Clients can of course be vulnerable and fragile. They bestow their trust generously and the work we do needs to be worthy of it. Once again, we can put our faith in the planets, the angles, the chart itself, along with our intention to *do no harm*.

When we prepare our forecasting notes we can see the critical processes playing out. We can trace the structure of the major cycles and understand the timeframes at work. Sometimes that alone can be incredibly comforting to hear – yes, last April and May things were hellish and I felt as if I was going under. Yes, four months ago I did survive my own personal storm. Looking back to discern the beginning of phases, as well as looking ahead to see their middle or end is all part of what forecasting requires. Again and again, it is how we deliver our understanding that makes all the difference. If someone has been through or is still going through some horribly difficult time, it is no use to pretend that all is fine, much less tell them to look on the bright side. What is needed is empathy and compassion. Listening, acknowledgement, acceptance, support. And that means allowing the time and space to honour whatever they are undergoing. You cannot make it better and you are not responsible for their pain, but you can be a witness and sometimes this alone is enough. They can be shown that they are not going mad and they are not being punished – they are participating in the act of becoming. If the snake never shed its skin or the seed never split, no growth would be possible. Life will shake us and up-end us and drag us through the mill, but astrology allows us a wider and deeper perspective. Within it we can find meaning and purpose.

It is useful to remind ourselves that we do not know what is going to happen. I do it all the time, telling my clients that I have no cast-iron assurances of what will be. Over the years I have moved from being insecure and burdened about this into feeling liberated. These days forecasting work allows me to experience a sense of expansion and creative openness which, treading softly, I proffer to my clients. If somehow I could swap this for being utterly certain of what would unfold, I would not choose to, since issuing proclamations from on high is not at all my goal. Rather, I aim to be alongside people and offer a wider perspective on their choices. Forecasting represents a dialogue about the potential stages ahead and an open discussion on the ways forward. The essence of astrological consultation for me is in offering a sense of how they already contain the horizons they have yet to experience.

In his *Letters to a Young Poet*, first written in the early 1900's but published decades later, the poet Rainer Maria Rilke beautifully described the sense of collaboration with our own growth.[5] He writes of our future as an idea which enters and lives within us, long before it ever takes place externally. This is a beautiful image and one which resonates deeply with the practice of astrology – after all, the myriad possibilities woven throughout our entire lives are somehow contained in the essence of that first moment.

Our being, our identity, and our core self can develop and continue to expand and blossom through all our days, if we choose to stay awake and alive to our possibilities and the callings of our heart, our soul. The more intimately we come to know ourselves, the more we can come to understand and accept what is reflected on the outside. One's life is representative of oneself – as indeed is one's astrological practice.

Forecasting can seem to open a Pandora's box of fate and free will, and it is up to each of us to investigate our own understanding of their interplay. In Pandora's myth, Hope was said to be the only thing remaining once all else had flown away and I think it is crucial to remember this. To offer forecasting that destroys hope is to betray astrology altogether. Yet neither can we dangle false hope, avoiding or denying the stones along the path. Sometimes the way will be hard – has to be hard – but we can try and equip and resource ourselves accordingly. A long hike can be possible with the right boots, or, as they say: there is no such thing as bad weather, just inappropriate clothing.

As Keats famously wrote in a letter to his friend Benjamin Bailey: 'I am certain of nothing but the holiness of the heart's affections and the truth of the imagination'.[6] The longer I practise, the more this statement seems to sum up my approach. As astrologers, I believe our role is to give as open, sensitively honest and truthfully imaginative an account as we can. It is not

## NEGOTIATING THE FUTURE

up to us to tell someone what they should or should not do. We can help to clarify their understanding of the terrain they are crossing, rather than try and insist on the path chosen. One person may well find the going harder than the next. In every journey, near or far, wherever we travel, we take ourselves.

### NOTES

1. A Solar Return chart is a chart which is calculated for the exact time that the Sun in its yearly voyage around the zodiac reaches the precise degree and minute of the natal Sun in a person's chart. It can occur on the actual birthday or a day either side. The chart symbolises the year in question.

2. Directions are a method of forecasting by which all the natal positions of the chart are moved forward by the same amount.

3. Progressions are a similar technique, but the amount of planetary movement reflects the actual cycles of the planets.

4. This old Babylonian fable tells how a merchant's servant flees Death in Baghdad only to meet at the allotted time in Samarra. It is retold by Liz Greene in *The Astrology of Fate*, p1.

5. Rainer Maria Rilke, *Letters to a Young Poet*, August 12 1904, trans. Stephen Mitchell (New York: Vintage, 1986).

6. John Keats, Letter to Benjamin Bailey, 22nd November 1817, in *The Letters of John Keats 1814-1821*, 2 vols, ed. H. E. Rollins (Cambridge: Cambridge University Press, 1958).

Chapter Four

# BECOMING YOUR OWN ASTROLOGER
## POLLY WALLACE

'Using astrology consciously, actively and constructively, we can discover ourselves and create ourselves in cooperation with universal forces.'[1]

The concept of becoming your own astrologer is both gentle and dynamic. It evokes a sense of natural development with space for dreaming and for exploring. At the same time, something tangible is happening as we build our astrological knowledge and skills. These two dimensions – inner journey and outer activity – are as integral to one another as the yin/yang symbols of oriental philosophy. Our relationship with astrology develops as we spiral between the invisible and the visible dimensions of our experience.

Astrology provides a fine role model for the process of becoming. Astrology's spectrum of connection embraces the depths of the psyche, the activity of the physical world, the drama of the sky. This abundant territory gives scope for astrology to re-invent itself – endlessly widening, never arriving. Since its emergence in the ancient world, astrology has evolved through successive transformations. Like tiny replicas of the master, we are likely to reflect this process, each in our own way, once we engage with astrology as a significant focus in our lives.

In this chapter my intention is to explore what it means to be involved in the process of becoming your own astrologer. I envisage it as an adventure that combines personal journeying with external goals and achievements. I hope to convey that, right from day one, every stage is a vital part of weaving astrology's pattern of meaning into our lives. I aim to describe how astrology offers a magical arena in which each one of us, whatever our level of expertise, is already becoming that unique entity – our own astrologer.

## INSPIRATION

As astrologers we are committed to the integrity of the natal chart. We honour this map of the sky as a blueprint for our life. It follows that the story of our own astrologer is in there somewhere – and has been since the moment we were born. Our astrologer may beam out at us confidently. More often its subtle spirit may be encased in the intricacies of our character and our experience. Either way, the task of becoming our own astrologer is about engaging what is already there. A master sculptor, sensing the unique qualities of a block of stone, applies himself to releasing the form within. Jacob Epstein explored this concept in pieces such as Maternity, a huge sculpture of a woman emerging from raw stone. This piece of work remains deliberately unfinished as though to accentuate her emergence as an on-going process.[2]

Astrology draws us into a process that is life-long and non-linear. We have emerged and we are still emerging; a snake displays one skin while future patterns are silently forming. Our progress is likely to be circuitous as we read and ponder, surf the net and pursue obscure corners of personal interest. Whatever we do enriches the material from which our own astrologer is created. Even our apparent mistakes – false starts, distractions, failures, errors of judgment – all count towards the unique astrologer we are becoming. Nothing is wasted. Our current astrological profile is the culmination of our progress so far. It is not the end of the story.

Central to astrology is the concept of change as the only constant. The planets, as they orbit the sun, transform the starry sky into a kaleidoscope of movement. Astrology translates this activity into its awareness of cycles. Initiative, activity and renewal succeed one another as night follows day. This glimpse of order may flicker into and out of view as we navigate our way through a tumult of astrological ideas. It illuminates the links between planetary activity and human experience. So far so good – intellectually. On a personal level, it's another matter. Planetary cycles can somehow morph into trip-wires that tip us way beyond our comfort zone. The ambition to become a qualified astrologer may seem straightforward enough. Several major planetary transits down the line, we may wonder how this clear plan convoluted itself into quite such an adventure!

Even more beguiling is the notion that our involvement with astrology may change us on a profound level. We discover that, in the guise of astrology, we have somehow formed a personal connection with the universe. Gradually we become more and more aware of a whole other dimension running alongside our daily lives. Events, both personal and collective, assume more significance. We may find ourselves adjusting our priorities, reformulating our intentions, adopting different strategies for achieving our goals. Shifts of awareness may range from subtle to seismic and it can be challenging to feel as if earlier dreams no longer satisfy, previous methods no longer work. The more we can trust this process and allow astrology to work on us, the more we appreciate how successive transformations are an inherent part of becoming our own astrologer.

Discovery by discovery astrology expands our awareness. A gentle learning curve turns out to be the foothills of a glorious range of mountains. Arriving at a plateau we think *ah, this is it*... until we look around and see the next slope beckon. Every curve of our progress brings its own gifts – the openness of beginner's mind, the compulsion to find out more, the satisfaction of building our skills, the joy of being able to share and develop them with our peers, clients and students. And all the time we can rely on astrology, the master magician, for continued inspiration as it becomes more apparent, or differently apparent, in the world around us.

We emerge into the world of astrology and we find that we are not alone. Our first tentative forays gather pace until, either physically or virtually, we become swept along with a tribe of like-minded souls. As excitement settles, we may experience a dichotomy; the impulse to assert our individuality nudges against our desire to identify with the group. So how can we nurture our emerging astrologer in ways that honour both our commitment to the collective and also our spirit of independence?

Already we may be aware that a plethora of issues cluster around astrology. These range from the sublime to the ridiculous. A middle ground of wise questions adds gravitas to our study and provides us with opportunities to identify and articulate our own viewpoint. An example – what is astrology? A straightforward question – the words are simple and their meaning is clear. Yet no two astrologers would give the same answer.

*Opera incompiuta* (William Girometti, 1998)

To set the ball rolling, this quotation from Jorge Luis Borges expresses my current view:

'The fact is that poetry is not the books in the library...it is the encounter of the reader with the book, the discovery of the book ...'[3]

When we substitute *astrology* for *poetry* this phrase suggests that our activity as astrologers is as vital to astrology as its wisdom is to us. Not long ago my answer would have been quite different and it is likely to change again as my astrological journey unfolds. I don't expect you to agree with me. I offer Borges' concept as an example of how the richness of astrology derives from the diversity of its participants. For astrology is a mystery. It evades capture into the net of a single concept. Compulsively we circle the mystery. Every aha moment encourages us — until a different insight flings our current ideas into disarray. But by now we are enthralled and so we start over again. As we find the ground beneath our feet, we strive to articulate our own ideas. We begin to express that 5th house entity, our own astrologer, who stands out clear and bright among the 11th house collective, our astrology tribe.

## ACTIVITY

From high in the sky a bird of prey spots a tiny creature in deepest woodland. The bird's vision combines wide overview with minute detail. Astrology does likewise. Spatially astrology's frame of reference is the cosmos; time-wise, astrology spans past, present and future. From this vast scope the astrologer can pinpoint a single moment in time and place. Such extreme viewpoints suggest tension — and invite exploration.

Nowadays we can explore to our heart's content. In most parts of the world the practice of astrology no longer breaks the law. Outbreaks of controversy remind us that there's no such thing as bad publicity. And I wonder — just how acceptable do we really want to be? Our marginalised position holds certain compensations. Astrology provides us with a platform from which to challenge mainstream thinking. It gives us a voice. There are even benefits hidden in the challenge from astrology's critics. Whenever we counter disapproval by leaping to the defence of astrology, we clarify our thinking in order to present our case. As we develop and articulate the stance of our own astrologer we realise how passionate we are about astrology. Mainstream society's lack of comprehension of astrology compels us to recognise ourselves as the guardians of powerful knowledge. And so, as we draw the gods into our lives, we become increasingly aware of the mystique of our commitment, the reality of sacred space. Invisible rites of passage run alongside our more obvious activity. Professional qualification may have taken the place of arcane hierarchies, yet the concept of initiation is still potent. It is inspiring to realise that, however harshly astrology is challenged, its innate truth supplies the power to endure.

The spirit of the age bestows on us freedom to learn and to practise astrology. Astrology spans many traditions. Imagine – down the centuries and across the globe – a carnival of astrologers emanating from all directions. Astrological literature, the internet and live groups connect us with mysterious ritual from early civilizations, magical practice of medieval times, vibrant ideas of traditional astrology and the sophistication of modern techniques. As we tailor our study to our own interests and needs, we can take our pick.

Our freedom is evident in the breadth of our resources. Saturn and Uranus, co-rulers of the Age of Aquarius, extend astrology's spectrum of knowledge from ancient belief systems to modern technological innovation. Saturn, guardian of time, oversees the revelation, restoration and preservation of historical systems of astrology. Under the aegis of Uranus, ingenuity and innovation enable these systems to proliferate and then be widely shared. Technology shrinks the world so that, wherever we live, we can gain the ideas and engage with the activities that fuel our adventure.

Astrology has become a fabulous emporium where we can explore our thinking, expand our knowledge, enrich our passion. As we develop our own relationship with astrology we're likely to become increasingly aware of our own astrology comfort zone. What really makes you tick? Do you yearn for the solitude of contemplative study or do you naturally gravitate to inter-active astrology events? Are you fascinated by mundane astrology or do you prefer the intimate subtleties of psychological astrology? Perhaps you express yourself best through the intricacies of complex techniques or do you find your voice in creativity and philosophy? Most important of all, do you notice how, from time to time, your own astrology comfort zone is liable to change? Take notice of what makes your own astrologer happy – knowing that every experience, every involvement in the world of astrology is a chance to enhance his/her persona and skills.

## THE NATAL CHART

A bird of prey soars – and then it pounces. Astrologers circle and gaze, surveying the wealth of resources around them. How and where to make the first inroad into finding out more about your own astrologer? A particular gem catches the light... The natal chart!

Astrology declares the unrepeatable quality of each moment of time. The natal chart captures this focus for the individual. No two natal charts are identical, no two people are the same. It follows that every astrologer is destined to become an astrologer like no other. By engaging with our natal chart we involve ourselves in a life-long programme of self-study. Our chart may offer clues about why we have been drawn to astrology. What is it about our character that resonates with astrology's challenge? How can we capitalise on the unique talents revealed to us by our natal chart? And, in return, how can we use these gifts to honour astrology?

From time to time I am asked, 'where does it show astrology in my chart?' I find myself reluctant to pin down astrology to any specific feature. For me, astrology is not something separate from the rest of life. It is a perspective on life. Astrology's guidance comes from the whole of our chart.

The first impression made by our chart may describe us as extrovert or introvert. Do we enjoy strutting our stuff in public or is happiness derived through private communion with our gods? The visual images of Marc Jones' Chart Shapings offer immediate access to main chart themes. These range from the Splash personality with its range of interests to the intense focus of a Bundle. One step away lie the elements. Their balance/imbalance can reveal our own unique combination of fiery enthusiasm, instinctive empathy, productive good sense, technical precision. And what about the general appearance of aspects? A preponderance of conjunctions may suggest intensity, powerful oppositions can indicate an affinity with relating.

Against a background of broad themes, the personal planets hold the essence of our character. From the Sun we gain understanding of our fundamental power while the Moon shows how this unfolds through the journey of our soul. Mercury highlights how our astrologer perceives the world while Venus symbolises where we find heart and meaning. Mars describes our astrologer's drive and motivation. Jupiter declares how personal vision develops into wisdom. Saturn is key to how our astrologer structures the complexities of his or her own experience. By inviting astrology into our personal lives, we begin to see ourselves from a whole new perspective. The natal chart may not provide direct answers but it can open a level of insight that allows our choices and decisions to become differently informed.

Through constant reference to our natal chart, we refine and deepen our understanding of our own astrologer. The emergence and progress of this astrologer can be traced through predictive techniques. At the time of our first encounter with our own astrologer were we shaken to the core? Were we elated to recognise the start of a fabulous adventure? Where was Pluto? Was Jupiter making a significant transit? What about Saturn? Perhaps his contact with our natal chart implied the presence of an enduring commitment. Saturn and Jupiter provide an interface of our astrologer with the outside world. Saturn's movement through natal 9th house could indicate desire for formal study of astrology while Jupiter's transit of natal 6th house may coincide with setting up professional practice. If transits show us the drama of tangible events and turning points – progressions can indicate the unfolding of a personal journey that deeply involves our own astrologer. For instance there could be a subtle change of tempo when progressed Sun moves from Aquarius to Pisces and Saturn relinquishes the reins into Jupiter's more easy-going hold.

The natal chart is a powerful secret with recognition of its symbols as the key. Think of how differently the same chart appears to someone who knows its symbols and someone who does not. One person recognises the chart's invitation, the other faces the blank stare of an impenetrable mystery. Astrology's symbols are amazing. At times they may lead us into what feels like alien territory – until we realise the symbols' constant presence is as reassuring as cats' eyes on a night-time road.

## RESOURCES

As we become involved with astrology, we tend to accumulate all sorts of resources. These include tangible objects and intellectual concepts. The obvious and the personal mingle together; an ephemeris is for everyone, the notes and pictures tucked inside it are idiosyncratic. Sound understanding of astrology's symbols is a requirement; an affinity for midpoints is optional.

Astrology may slip seamlessly into and around our existing life-style. And then one day we start to notice astrology books lurking under the furniture and pages of strange hieroglyphics meandering through our home. Sooner or later astrology demands its own space. A corner of the bedroom, a purpose-built cabin in the garden – anywhere is okay so long as there is room for astrology's paraphernalia and the potential for solitude. In this place we can immerse ourselves in the mystery of astrology's symbolism and the power of astrology's truth. For it is our involvement with astrology that brings about the transformation of a workaday place into sacred space.

Astrology's paraphernalia includes the tools of our trade. Imagine the range and variety of tool-kits that could contain such personalised treasure. An exhibition of our dream tool-kits would be a motley crew – decorative, workmanlike, organised, over-flowing – each one reflecting the unique aspirations of its owner. More seriously, there is also our metaphorical tool-kit. This is composed of our astrological knowledge, relevant skills, qualifications and achievements. It also serves as a sketchbook for our plans and projects – with plenty of blank pages for all those elusive ideas that keep our dreams alive.

Different skills come centre-stage during our journey from apprentice to master. There is no prescribed order for this as it is motivated by the evolution of our own astrologer. Our tool-kit grows with us, changing to reflect our astrologer's current phase. It offers tangible proof of the adventure of our astrologer. From time to time we may like to sort out our tool kit. This may reveal long-lost treasures tucked into the corners. It is also an opportunity to distinguish between what is working well for us and what has already served its purpose. As we jettison what no longer works, we create space for new tools.

It is often helpful to choose one main system for learning astrology and to make this central to our tool-kit. This opens a clear pathway to follow. It also offers a label that begins to distinguish our own astrologer. Astrology provides a range of systems, from ancient to modern, from which we can choose a basis for our study. It may be provident to begin with a branch of astrology that is relatively well-known. Nowadays psychological astrology and traditional astrology are both popular while spiritual astrology appears to be enjoying a renaissance. By choosing to base our learning on a system that has stood the test of time, we maximise our chance of accessing sound teaching, abundant resources and a vibrant peer group to nourish our involvement.

Involvement with astrology aligns us with our tribe. It is also a personal adventure, vitalised by the impulse to try out a range of ideas, to take a risk, to dare to be different. Such exploration develops our insight into our own abilities and affinities. This goes hand in hand with the honesty to recognise what does or does not really work for us. We are likely to become increasingly realistic, more and more selective. We recognise when viewpoints, systems and techniques, however highly praised, do not fit into our own way of thinking. We retain whatever is essential – and discard what is superfluous. As we exercise the freedom not to do everything, we develop confidence and our own astrologer becomes more empowered.

## OUTCOMES

Astrology is not an obvious path, nor an easy one. Yet once we've found it, any element of choice seems to fade away. Our world takes on fresh meaning; a pied piper is passing by... Astrology's role in our life may seem to go through changes. This beloved confidant and wise ally can, at times, morph into the most demanding of teachers. One thing that remains unchanged is the constancy of astrology's presence somewhere in our lives.

Our commitment to astrology extends its influence to all areas of our life. We see the world otherwise and we take into account different considerations. Time re-invents itself. We discover an alternative to the rule of calendars and clocks. The year becomes the cycle of the Sun, unfolding graciously through its seasonal pattern. The month transforms into phases of the Moon. We realise each weekday has a planetary ruler and each hour belongs to a meaningful sequence. Calendars and clocks adjust to being useful devices that no longer monopolise our experience of time.

As for the planets – their cycles form the beating heart of astrology. Ephemeris in hand, we make connections between movement of the planets in the sky and events down here. The ups and downs of our own experience illustrate the spectrum of impact contained within these planetary cycles. Synchronicity – lovely word, magical concept! Synchronicity adds vitality to our theoretical understanding of 'as above, so below'. Something occurs that takes us by surprise – we check out the planets and it begins to make sense. We dream of some event...it happens...and then we find the astrology matches. Casual references to coincidence dwindle in the light of astrology's affinity with meaningful cycles, serious patterns. It is as if our life has developed its own sixth sense – a dimension of meaning. Increasingly we make sense of our own experience, and of the world around us, in terms of astrology's paradigm of significance.

Sooner or later we realise that not only do we think differently from the rest of the world, but also we think differently from other astrologers. It's likely that, right from the start, our involvement with astrology has developed hallmarks of its own. We each come to astrology bearing the special gifts and the unique scars of our personal history. We each involve ourselves differently with astrology. We each envisage our future astrologer through aspirations that range from casual interest to major ambition. We have different approaches to astrology – passionate or rational, articulate or reflective. As with any important commitment, our involvement goes through stages and phases. We can compare notes with our peers, we can find common ground – but our relationship with astrology is ultimately our own.

Many of us want to become astrologers – right? This dream is a like vast umbrella, extending its protective arch over the whole gamut of astrological motivation and ambition. Astrology is a quest. Self-understanding and personal empowerment are likely to underpin our progress. More boldly we may hope to glimpse the meaning of life, the nature of the universe. Practical ambitions could centre on helping people, researching diverse cultures, creatively exploring the realms of astrology... As we develop our own ideas, opinions, attitudes, affinities and skills we find our own voice and our own style. A distinctive approach fuels our engagement with one another and inspires our unique contribution to the world of astrology and beyond.

Astrology's various systems offer choice and diversity. Astrology also gives us the chance to develop whatever it is we love to do. A studious programme can be enhanced by less direct methods of progress using creative imagination, ritual and experiential methods. Happily we discover many ways for imagination to keep us connected with the gods of astrology.

Further enrichment comes from combining astrology with other systems of thought – psychology, philosophy, tarot, kabbalah, creative arts, languages, literature. The list is as endless as our own predilections. All sorts of opportunities may further define our own astrologer. Once our astrological persona becomes visible we may be asked to give a talk, write an article, teach a class, lead a group. This can seem daunting, yet with astrology as our focus and guide we may find a courage that we never knew we had. Unwittingly we have become an ambassador for astrology. As we articulate our own ideas about astrology, we realise that this elusive entity, our own astrologer, has become real.

Visible goals may fuel our motivation and provide a valid means of self-assessment. Our success in the 10th house realm of public achievement is valuable. It boosts our confidence – and maybe our income. While the world sees us gaining skills and qualifications, our inner experience of becoming our own astrologer is likely to be even more rewarding. As with other powerful relationships, there comes a point where we identify ourselves with the words, I am an astrologer. The magic of commitment and the empowerment of belonging works like a charm. We recognise who we are and we realise that we can take our place in a timeless tradition. Our professional pathway and our inner development are intrinsically connected. Outwardly our own astrologer is likely to gain a wider and deeper knowledge of astrology, in principle and in practice. Inwardly this is supported by an empowered sense of self and a deeper commitment to our own relationship with astrology. This balance of yang and yin flowers into a re-vitalised approach to our own experience of, well – anything and everything. It is exhilarating to find our astrological role emerge, fascinating to watch how this changes.

## *MAPPA MUNDI*

As time goes by the process of becoming our own astrologer takes twists and turns that strengthen our relationship with astrology. We develop a profound connection with our natal chart. We comprehend how this astrological map encompasses our character, our life and our experience. It takes into account the whole of our life – past, present and future. It shows our journey and it tells our story. It is our own *mappa mundi*.

A mappa mundi is a medieval world map. Also known as an estoire, it tells the story of the world. Long before maps were used as an aid to navigation, their remit was to give a view of the whole of life and all of knowledge. *Mappae mundi* contained far more than a modern map. They came in all shapes and sizes and were packed with information: history,

## THE JOURNEY THROUGH ASTROLOGY

*Mappa Mundi* (from Jean Mansel's *La Fleur des Histoires*, Valenciennes, 1459-1463)

classical learning and legend, the wonders of nature, stories from the Bible. An assortment of creatures and mythical beasts pranced through *mappa mundi*'s world. Everything was there...real and imaginal.

A *mappa mundi* seeks to interpret the world in spiritual as well as geographical terms. The natal chart carries a similar intention; we look for significance in its catalogue of celestial events. Astrology's map creates a paradigm that illuminates our experience. Its symbols are constant yet nothing stays the same. The natal chart is multi-faceted. We cannot see the whole of it at the same time. Different facets catch the light, bringing our awareness to a relevant point of focus, just as the *mappa mundi* sought to shed light on a world that was in process of discovery.

By viewing the natal chart as a *mappa mundi* that holds the essence of our story, we see how the adventure of becoming our own astrologer is intricately tied up with the life-long journey of becoming more of ourselves. Each chart or map is profoundly individual. As guardian of our personal *mappa mundi*, our own astrologer has the freedom of the kingdom this map describes.

## OUR OWN ASTROLOGER

The concept of becoming our own astrologer projects us into the future. What sort of astrologer do we aspire to be? How can we move towards this aspiration? Once we sense the form of our own astrologer within the marble of our character, we realise that the process is already underway. We chip into the casing, newly conscious of an intention to find and to liberate our own astrologer.

Our passion for astrology inspires us with a spirit of adventure. As we pursue a range of astrological ideas and activities, we become increasingly aware of the individuality inherent in our life-style and our predilections. We tap into our intuition, conscious of how our inner life motivates and sustains the development of our relationship with astrology. Imagination conjures up a wealth of roles for our own astrologer's unique style of combining astrological skill with personal talent. We develop confidence in our own viewpoint, our own ideas.

Our character, vision, experience, abilities and life-style create a unique stance from which to make an individual contribution to astrology – and to the world. Interaction between inner journey and outer activity creates the spiral along which our own astrologer can combine private harmony with evident skills. James Hillman captures the complexity of becoming into the weave of a single sentence:

'I am different from everyone else and the same as everyone else; I am different from myself ten years ago and the same as myself ten years ago; my life is a stable chaos, chaotic and repetitive both, and I can never predict what tiny, trivial bit of input will result in a huge and significant output...'[4]

As Hillman suggests, our way forward is likely to be uneven – paved with contradictions, lit by surprises. Change is the only constant. The astrologer you are today is likely to be different from the one you were five years ago or five years into the future. Yet always you are the same person, living out the same chart as you explore the timeless realm of your own *mappa mundi*.

### NOTES

1. Tracey Marks, *The Astrology of Self-Discovery* (US & Canada: CRCS Publications, 1985), p.3.

2. Grace Brockington, Jacob Epstein, *Sculptor in Revolt* www.artandarchitecture.org.uk/insight/brockington_epstein/brockington_epstein04.html

3. Jorge Luis Borges, lecture entitled 'Poetry', from the collection *Seven Nights*, trans. by Eliot Weinberger (New York: New Directions, 2009).

4. James Hillman, *The Soul's Code* (New York: Warner Books, 1996), p.140.

Chapter Five
# PERILS AND PITFALLS ON THE PATH: ETHICS IN ASTROLOGICAL PRACTICE
## DEBORAH MORGAN

Let me start at the beginning. Once upon a time, when I was tiny and the world was large, populated by giant grown-ups and monsters hiding under the bed, I used to look out of my bedroom window at the moon and feel at peace. I would sit in the garden and watch the sun rise, peak, and fall back towards the horizon, shedding light upon my reality. The rhythms of the world rotated around me, and I, a little girl who loved to read, imagine and dream, centred myself gratefully within the eternal cosmic dance. Jupiter was my friend. Retrograde, in Pisces in the 5th house, Jupiter in my natal chart showed me inner worlds of meaning whilst I sat under a tree by the stream at the bottom of the garden. I might not have travelled a lot as a child, but Jupiter took me places. One of these journeys was to a local bookshop when I was 12, in the year of my first Jupiter return. I picked up a copy of *Linda Goodman's Sun Signs*, and began to read. I was on my way. I have an astrological narrative of my life, bound in to my other stories which I use to make sense of my life.

To me, my life with astrology is interwoven with my attempts to answer big questions. Why am I here? What is my purpose? Why do I, one person amongst billions on one planet amidst a cosmic sea of colour, light, and sparkling, half-glimpsed stars in the brilliant heavens, feel impelled to work daily with these huge mysteries of life? How can a path be established through the sublunary world of the neoplatonist tradition, by an individual soul inhabiting the *Anima Mundi*, the Soul of the World? Astrology can place a soul in context. We are individuals, but we are not alone. We are each unique, yet linked in some Neptunian, undefinable yet recognisable way. And, as astrologers, we may be more aware of the expansive possibilities, to use a good Jupiterian phrase, of our outlook, situations and relationships. We can sense, intuit and discern other meanings as well as their outer manifestation.

I mentioned other narratives. Big stories, little stories, very personal stories, Mercury speaking and guiding me through Saturnian experiences and Jupiter helping me to see a way forward. I often didn't notice, but they were still there. I'd always thought of these as being mine, albeit with a mythological edge, taking my cue from the work of Joseph Campbell and the idea of the hero's journey through life. By using mythology, we can make sense of our situations. Of course, Freud, Jung, and other psychoanalysts went considerably deeper into this than my early teenage self, but my 12th house loved the concept of the interrelation between past and present.

## SYMBOLS AND STORIES: PERSONAL TALES, CULTURAL NARRATIVES AND MYTHICAL ARCHETYPES

Let me jump cut to my mid-thirties. Now wiser and a bit battle worn after an eventful Saturn Return at twenty nine, I had re-evaluated my priorities and decided I wanted more from life than low-paid employment and a nasty sick feeling in the mornings when it was time to get up.

I went to university as a mature student to study English, and was introduced to different literary theories. In a nutshell, these attempt to illuminate how meaning is constructed from a text and how symbols function. Obviously, there are some neat parallels here with astrological interpretation, but this expanded the focus from the personal to the political. Jupiter began to stir.

I learned how society constructed meaning and power; how cultures maintained and expanded control. In my postmodernist theory classes I saw how, in a post-industrial age, the production of knowledge has become more significant than the manufacture of material goods. Civilisations made big stories called metanarratives which were an intrinsic part of this. Now Mercury's ears pricked up.

Saturn would like a concrete example here to bring theory down to earth. One metanarrative in the Middle Ages in Europe was the Catholic Church, a powerful political, religious and spiritual authority with an extensive power over all members of feudal society. A later metanarrative was that of the British Empire, which employed social constructions of race, morality, religion and nationalism to control millions.

Although postmodernism ostensibly rejected the metanarrative in contemporary society, suggesting instead that cultural relativism was on the rise, it's hard, at least to my mind, to think of the technological and financial power of Google and other multi-nationals, the certainty of fundamentalist monotheistic beliefs and the continued prevalence of rationalist, empiricist science as not being examples of metanarratives. I would argue that some older metanarratives have been replaced by newer, more effective versions better suited to our times. I can't claim this as my own idea as literary theorists beat me to it years ago, but academic study showed me a new way of looking at the world. As a child I had felt attuned to the natural world and its rhythms; as an adult I tuned in to the collective tides of a capitalist society.

So far, so good. It made sense. I could see it. I even really liked bits of it, in an academic, intellectual sort of way. I admired the way Mercury danced through the pages in a dazzling, bewildering display of linguistic virtuosity. So many ideas, sparking half-caught thoughts that slipped through my mind before I could put them into words. I enjoyed the debates, the disagreements between theorists and philosophers; the openness of the discussions. Like astrology, it showed me that as individuals we navigate through a world not of our own making, and yet we are deeply connected to our environment. The dual nature of Mercury signposted choices, divisions and binary options in the world of ideas and symbols while Jupiter illuminated their moral dilemmas, underlying beliefs and moral repercussions. Jupiter's role as the wise guide brought the ethical implications of such systems of thought into my mind, and I was fascinated by this inner vision.

But it didn't set my heart on fire like astrology did, nor did my pulse race at the thought of settling down with a good book of post-colonial theory. One night I dreamed that I was working on a chart, entering the glyphs and starting my interpretation. A feeling of joy suffused me as I looked at the all-encompassing chart wheel. Here, it seemed, was what brought me happiness.

I enrolled with the Faculty the summer after I graduated during my third Jupiter return and gained my Diploma at my fourth Jupiter return. At this point I was formally introduced to Jupiter in a new guise when I signed the Faculty's Code of Ethics.

## TRAVELS WITH MERCURY AND JUPITER: EVALUATING KNOWLEDGE AND CHOOSING A PATH

By this time I was seeing clients and had an inkling of what might crop up in the consulting room. I had seen one client burst into tears at the casual mention of the word 'mother' and sensed that what I might say could have considerable impact. Misunderstandings could easily develop. I grew anxious that I might unintentionally injure my clients' feelings and autonomy. But, if I'm honest (and Jupiter would like me to be) I saw ethics as a bit of an afterthought. I wasn't acting unethically, but they weren't at the forefront of my mind.

According to the *Oxford English Dictionary*, the word 'ethics' is defined as either: 'Moral principles that govern a person's behaviour or the conducting of an activity' or 'the branch of knowledge that deals with moral principles'.[1] Knowledge, morals and practice are entwined and inseparable in these sentences, which are heavy with the presence of the social planets, Jupiter and Saturn.

I take the definitions to mean that while the practice of ethics may be determined by individual morality, these principles are shaped by the beliefs of that person which are, in turn, shaped by the culture and world in which he or she lives. In other words, the metanarratives of the late 20th century have played a huge role in determining my moral outlook, as have my experiences of life in this culture and my spiritual beliefs that recognise that there is more to life than quotidian routine. In turn, these affect my astrological practice and ethics. Writing this, I think of the different forms the mythological Jupiter took to interact with mortals in order to bring heavenly wisdom to the physical world.

The story of Philemon and Baucis[2] is a good example of this. This classical myth from Ovid's *Metamorphoses* narrates how Jupiter and Mercury disguised themselves as peasants and visited a small town, seeking hospitality from the inhabitants. Only one household took them in, comprising an old couple named Philemon and Baucis, who quickly realised the true identity of their guests. Jupiter rewarded them by granting their one wish, that they would die together when the time came, as they could not bear to be separated by death.

I'm not suggesting that Jupiter will strike us down if we tie ourselves in an ethical tangle during a consultation. After all, 'to err is human, to forgive, divine'.[3] But sometimes it can feel as if there are more persons present in the consulting room than just the astrologer and client. Here, acting as an intermediary between the heavens and the temporal concerns of the individual, in a liminal position between worlds, astrologers may find themselves negotiating a delicate path between current events in clients' lives, their beliefs and the overall story arc of their lives. Working with progressions and planetary cycles can provide a context for their prevailing concerns, and clients may start to make connections between their past, present, and what they may wish for their future.

Nimble Mercury, the messenger of the gods who can travel wherever he wishes, has helped me negotiate a path between these inner and outer worlds. Note that the two gods travelled together in Ovid's tale, wisdom and words walking through the town to find a house that would take them in, knocking on doors but receiving no answer – except one. Mercury appears in his role as companion and guide, walking with Jupiter to facilitate his search.

It may be that it is not so much that the gods don't listen to us as that we rarely take the time to listen to them. An astrological consultation can provide a rare opportunity to do so.

Although ethics are often associated with Jupiter, in practice Saturn also comes into the picture. Ovid refers to Mercury and Jupiter having to stoop to cross the threshold of the old couple's house; hinting at initiation into a new way of being, of having to fit with external circumstances in order to enter a new realm. They are invited in and welcomed by the elderly pair, and honoured as guests deserving the best despite their apparently lowly status. There is a theme of rebirth for both the gods entering the home and Philemon and Baucis as the latters' worldly reputation undergoes a considerable shift as a consequence of the divine visit. Their wish, that they should die together, ensured that they crossed the final boundary between life and death together.

*Mercury and Jupiter in the House of Philemon and Baucis* (Jacob van Oost)

Originally identified as poor, old, and as knowing their 'duty to gods and men',[4] Philemon and Baucis conform to the established social norms of kindliness and friendship. They practise their principles with generosity and concern for others at a cost to themselves. This is rewarded by Jupiter. While the rest of the town is flooded by a deluge sent by him, the couple's house is transformed into a temple to Jupiter. The couple serve as temple guardians for the rest of their lives, venerating Jupiter and providing sanctuary for his worshippers.

Remember that Philemon and Baucis weren't expecting Jupiter and Mercury to turn up; they hadn't tidied up or straightened the sofa cushions, hadn't hunted through the classical equivalent of the freezer for something that would make a presentable meal. They responded in a manner that reflected their heartfelt belief that strangers should be welcomed, well-fed, and reassured that all was well. They were even prepared to kill their most valuable possession, a goose, in order to feed their guests. They lived and breathed their beliefs and principles and their behaviour reflected these so clearly that they impressed two deities.

PERILS AND PITFALLS ON THE PATH: ETHICS IN ASTROLOGICAL PRACTICE

## SATURN'S SUPPORT: EXPRESSING INNER BELIEFS WITHIN AN ETHICAL PARADIGM

While Jupiter appears as the main protagonist in this story Saturn provides the framework of structure, doorways and the restructuring of Philemon and Baucis' house into a temple symbolising the construction of a life based on firm ethical principles. Jupiter and Saturn, assisted by Mercury, bring divine inner knowledge down to the physical world and manifest its gifts for all to see.

Ethics can be established in an outer form too. Subscribing to an external Code of Ethics manifests our inner beliefs, our trust in our talents and abilities, and with astrology, places these in a metaphysical context that envelops practitioner and client in a divine context. It marks our own crossing over the threshold, framing, guiding and supporting us. Whether we see this Saturn structure as limiting or empowering can say much about our relationship with the planets as well as our attitude towards ethics in a formal sense.

In my belief and experience, ethics provide a framework in which astrologers can feel held, secure in their practice and underpinned by philosophical beliefs. In my practice I feel supported by the Faculty Code and more confident in client work. Ethics aren't necessarily fixed or rigid. I know that mine have evolved as my personal experience, understanding and astrological life have deepened and continued, with client work producing some very real challenges to my views. Personal perceptions are key: are ethics a restriction on a free thinking, open-minded astrologer or indicators of professional boundaries?

I said earlier that I had an inkling of what could arise in a one-to-one consultation, but I simply never expected the sheer range of life situations, spiritual opinions and personal philosophies shown by clients, though I had previously worked in a one-to-one role as a student advisor at several universities. I thought I had heard most things, but no student ever asked me if he should marry a particular person as one fiancé asked privately about his wife-to-be, after I'd elected a wedding chart for the happy couple. Nor had a student asked me to go through her husband's natal chart and forecasting for his entire life to tell her about every single relationship he'd ever had as she was convinced he was having an affair.

What does a jobbing astrologer, reasonably confident in her ability to handle the astrological techniques and extremely fond of chart work, do when confronted with the complexities of human experience and sometimes extreme emotional distress? Such times illustrate the support that ethics can provide, and guide us to a safe harbour.

I learned that being able to say no to a client's request because it contravened ethics can be a great gift, and provide the chance to explore why the person is asking. Ethical ideas aren't just about personal morality, what I think or feel is right or wrong, but about transgression, boundaries and social and personal norms established on the collective level. Personal stories and metanarratives interweave. Ethics help the astrologer to negotiate a path through a maze of individual dilemmas and concerns, like Ariadne unrolling a guiding thread through the Minotaur's maze of perceptions, relationships, longings and loss.

Subscribing to a formal Code of Ethics can offer comfort in such situations. It can feel easier to tell a client that a request contravenes the Faculty's Code of Ethics rather than feel required to defend this view on a personal level. I was once asked if I had told another client something in a consultation. Being able to say that this was confidential under the Faculty's Code of Ethics was a huge relief, taking a weight of personal pressure off me. While exerting emotional pressure is one thing, asking someone to go against professional ethics is another, and clients, like most people, are unlikely to expect us to break professional boundaries. This protects them too as most people, I would suggest, wouldn't wish to consult a person who didn't take professional rules seriously. And if they did wish us to do so, we, as astrologers, can choose whether or not to work with that person.

This brings me to another area of ethics. While astrologers generally, I believe, genuinely wish to support their clients as fully as possible, there are healthy limits that can protect both from feeling vulnerable. A client who rings frequently or seeks 'permission' to go on holiday, as one client early in my astrological career did, may be expressing a wish for confirmation and approval rather than astrological insights. I was surprised when this happened – why would anyone need my say-so before booking a holiday? This phone call came out of the blue weeks after this client's consultation and I wasn't expecting to hear from her.

A conversation about using astrology as supporting information rather

# PERILS AND PITFALLS ON THE PATH: ETHICS IN ASTROLOGICAL PRACTICE

*A Reading Woman Tries in Vain to Stop Chronos as He Passes By*

than the Delphic oracle followed. From something as simple as holiday plans arose an in-depth discussion of fate and free-will and the role of trust in independent decision-making, reflecting astrology's potential for showing the intrinsic philosophical meaning behind overt actions. It illustrates how an ethical issue can arise seemingly from nowhere. That was how I dealt with this matter, as I began to extricate myself from what I considered to be this client's unhealthy reliance on both me and astrology. I was very uncomfortable with the role I felt I had been assigned, reluctant to carry responsibility for another's choices when aware of my limitations. Some astrologers may enjoy this, but I knew I didn't. I wanted to work alongside my clients assisting their journey of self-discovery, not be placed on a pedestal only to turn out later, in my client's eyes, to have feet of clay. I suggested that my client did as she wished.

## OUTER PERCEPTIONS AND INNER THOUGHTS: JUPITER'S WISDOM AND MERCURY'S MYTHS

Going back in retrograde fashion to metanarratives, collectively astrologers can be seen as standing outside social norms. It's fair to say that someone desperate for social approval, high income and commensurate professional and public status is unlikely to set up an astrological practice anytime soon. Astrologers are often grouped with fortune tellers, psychics, tarot readers and other undesirable outsiders (at least, undesirable in the eyes of a rationalist and materialist culture). Clients may unconsciously project these views onto the astrologer, impacting on their perception of the astrologer's honesty, conduct and professional reputation. A client may think, if great scientific minds reject astrology as superstition, why should an astrologer be skilled, genuine and sincere?

Astrologers can feel marginalised, denigrated, patronised and ignored. By daring to stand outside convention, the presence of astrology and astrologers after thousands of years of practice and hundreds of years of Enlightenment rationalism may be irritants to contemporary society. Yet, alongside this big story of Western material certainty is a counter narrative of spirituality, soul-searching and divine discontent amongst many seeking a more meaningful and connected way of living. We may wish to be recognised as individuals, but we probably don't want to be alone.

The low status of astrology in a materialistic Western culture can be used as a defence by clients if they prefer not to accept the information offered. Our words can be dismissed as lucky guesses, cold reading or the result of background research prompting the intriguing question of why apparently reluctant clients consult an astrologer in the first place. 'Anyone could say

# PERILS AND PITFALLS ON THE PATH: ETHICS IN ASTROLOGICAL PRACTICE

that' sniffed one Scorpio Ascendant client when I, as an introductory remark, suggested that she might value her privacy. Yet in other cultures the figures of the magus, shaman and spiritual guide have been honoured as a calling, with the person acting as an intermediary between the earth and the divine. Some clients recognise these roles, others do not. Dealing with both types in a way that serves them can be a challenge.

The burden of expectation can be keenly felt by an astrologer, especially when adventuring into professional practice for the first time. It can be confusing to feel that suddenly one is found wanting if unable to confirm that the new boyfriend of a fortnight is a soul-mate or not. I once had a client when I worked on a now defunct phone-line who rang to ask if she'd got the job for which she had just attended an interview. Looking at her forecasting, it didn't look hopeful, and I gently suggested that the astrological trends appeared more centred on other areas of her life.

'But I deserve a bit of luck,' she protested, 'so I should get it'.

A quick look at a horary chart didn't alter my opinion. I was tempted to say that she was the one who had gone to the interview and probably had a better idea about her success or otherwise than I did. Biting my tongue and reminding myself that I had a twenty minute maximum to endure for the consultation, I referred back to the astrology and tried to open up a discussion about career goals and fulfilment.

'Well, have I got it or haven't I?' the client snapped. 'I don't think it seems very likely, but I am just looking at the astrology here and may be misinterpreting a factor', I answered, my Libra Ascendant moving into tact overdrive. There was silence, followed by a sigh of exasperation.

She left a one-star review on the website and added that I hadn't answered her question properly. I could see her point. I hadn't said what she wanted to hear, and it may have seemed as though I was reluctant to give a straight yes or no answer. In such situations it can feel impossible to act honestly without irritating the client. I could have told her yes and she'd have gone away happy, but then might not have got the position and considered me incompetent or dishonest. Or she might have been delighted with her new job and her consultation.

I still wonder if she got it or not.

The opposite situation, of a client taking every word as a pearl of profound truth that has been revealed by a person of considerable spirituality, possessing breath-taking insight into their life, can be equally disconcerting. Another phone-line client, having just provided her birth information, recounted a story about her operation for an ingrown toenail three years earlier.

She finished with the comment: 'But I expect you know that already'. I couldn't think of anything to say as I stared at her chart. Was I meant to be able to see that? Was there something wrong with me because I couldn't? Why did she think I'd know? Eventually I managed to say, quite truthfully, that I didn't cover health matters. The difference between then and now is that at that time I felt I'd failed because I hadn't seen something the client believed I should have done. Now I think, having been forced to do so by this situation, that I don't do these as I have no medical background and don't feel competent to do so. It's one of those things, like going to the gym or drinking Guinness, that I just don't do. There's a big difference. The former was an emotional response, a lunar flare of anxiety and failure, the latter a mercurial, reasoned statement. Both conform to Jupiter's fondness for truth and say the same thing. But I'm sure I'd never have thought this through without that client's phone call.

Consciously or not, we will act in alignment with our ethics. Personally, recognising my limitations frees clients to contact another astrologer who might be able to address their concerns, and avoids me floundering around feeling that I'm making a mess of the consultation.

Clients can come out with extremely personal information during their consultations. One client burst into tears over her anxiety that her partner was having an affair. A month or so later, a different client excitedly told me about her new partner, how wonderful he was, how attentive, and how his live-in partner didn't understand or deserve him. As she talked, providing considerable information about him, Mercury began making connections and I realised that her new partner was the first client's unfaithful long-term partner.

I began to feel a bit queasy, worrying that my face was showing my thoughts and remembering painful times from my life. I tried not to fidget; to keep my body language still while my mind raced ahead. I tried to keep my voice neutral while inside I felt truly torn between her joy at finding love and my earlier client's genuine distress. Maybe I was wrong about the situation, but I didn't think I was.

This isn't the only time when I've felt considerable dissonance between my ideas about relationships and those of clients. I suspect that people in blissful partnerships don't consult astrologers, but the astrologer's role can be a difficult one at times. It is not for me to say how clients should run their lives nor do I wish to do so, but the consulting room can be a crucible for intense plutonian feelings as well as mercurial dialogue. Conversation can trigger memories, impressions and sensations for both client and astrologer. The transit will express itself differently for both, but the emotional echoes can occur very quickly and their intensity can be unexpected. Being aware of the speed with which feelings can be activated can be a good idea. Saturn can be a true friend here, maintaining professional boundaries while allowing a doorway through which the chart can speak.

Knowing that my ethics mean complete confidentiality for clients ensures that the consulting room can be a safe space where they feel supported, held and confident that their words will go no further. It can provide the chance to admit to themselves profound insights about their lives. It also means that I keep information to myself and thus separate myself from any further involvement in clients' lives and any feeling of obligation to inform one client of the words of another one.

Sometimes it can feel as though the client is daring the astrologer for a judgement, as if they feel they're being naughty and see the astrologer as an authority figure to criticise them for bad behaviour. I'm really not into that. One client having an affair pushed hard at this boundary while I wondered why she appeared to want this reaction. If she had really wanted someone to condemn her, why not ring up his wife who might be more obliging in this respect? Perhaps she was playing with this role in a space where it was safe to do so. I don't know, but I felt uncomfortable. I have always seen my role as supportive and working alongside the client, and felt troubled by this apparent imbalance in our perceptions.

Others simply want information. One client asked when her forecasting showed a good time to have an affair as her husband was really boring. Another wanted to know if her husband was salting money away in a secret account as she thought he was planning to leave her and wanted to make sure that she was financially secure. Although there was probably a lengthy emotional story behind both of these enquiries, the clients were focused on these specific areas and we worked together on these.

THE JOURNEY THROUGH ASTROLOGY

## JUPITER RETURNS: ABSORBING THE WISDOM OF THE PAST INTO THE PRESENT

I do not wish to imply that I have reached some mythical pinnacle, from which I can survey my earlier life in astrology and spot the errors in my consultative methodology and life in neat, regular steps up the mountain. It has not been a straight path. When I look back I see Jupiter breaking through, shaking everything up and encouraging me to get out there and learn more whether I wanted to or not and, as befits its natal retrograde motion, process my inner understanding. Nor can I say that I simply thought about ethical considerations when it was time for me to sign the Faculty Code of Ethics.

Instead, it has been more like a pilgrimage that zigzagged, took detours through unattractive marshland and abandoned factory sites, went round in circles for years at a time and every so often nudged forward into a meadow or a brick wall. For years, from about seventeen to my midthirties, astrology was absent, and I missed it. I couldn't have given a name to my longing for reconnection. Then, after my dream about working on a chart and my conscious rededication to what William Lilly called 'this heavenly knowledge of the stars',[5] I came home. I was back with Jupiter, sitting under the tree, watching the natural world go round.

I can't pretend that I suddenly started handling life better. I fumbled through my forecasting, tripped over the opportunities offered by transits and beat myself up about it. Being older, and hopefully a little bit wiser, I believe that life can be messy and full of loose ends, relationships that test our mettle or didn't work out; that there can be joy, beauty and delight as well as trauma and grief. This spills over into my ethics and astrological practice. Life can be tough, confusing and feel out of balance, and a neutral listener, who does not condemn or judge, doesn't tell the client what they should do or ask how on earth they ended up in a situation, can provide considerable support and empowerment for the client.

And in the background, ever turning, the luminaries and planets move on their cosmic paths, waiting for us to take time to listen and watch. The energy tides of sunrise and sunset wash over us daily, even in our curtain-drawn centrally-heated city homes that shut the world out. We travel through our environment by car, train or tram, obeying the social rules and keeping to our timetables even if the trains don't. But sometimes we might gaze out of the window and daydream a bit, or go places in our dreams. And in these quiet moments, the gods may knock, and, like Philemon and Baucis, we might choose to answer and accept their gifts.

## NOTES

1. http://www.oxforddictionaries.com/definition/english/ethics accessed 17th December 2014.

2. Ovid, translated by David Raeburn, *Metamorphoses: A New Verse Translation* (London: Penguin Classics, 2004) [hereafter *Metamorphoses*:], pp.324-328.

3. Alexander Pope, *An Essay on Criticism Part II* (London: Penguin Classics, 2011), p.17.

4. *Metamorphoses*, p.324.

5. William Lilly, *Christian Astrology* (Abingdon: Astrology Classics, 2004), p.xxxi.

Chapter Six

# ENGAGING AND DIALOGUING WITH ANOTHER PERSON IN AN ASTROLOGICAL CONSULTATION

## LINDSAY RADERMACHER

### THE JOURNEY OF THE ASTROLOGICAL 'CONSULTANT'

To journey as an astrological 'consultant' is to learn – through the extraordinary filter of astrology – about oneself, and about other people. This occurs via those who come to you to engage in work on their birth charts. It is an exchange of being, rather than of knowing. Above all, it is a meeting.

The word 'consultation' suggests an asymmetric encounter. One person 'consults'; the other is 'consulted'. The one approached seems to be in a stronger, more knowledgeable position; the one approaching seems to be in need, less knowledgeable. Yet most practising astrologers learn that the astrological consultation is not like this at all. It may be difficult to define what goes on in the dialogue between astrologer and client, but – whatever it is – there is an inherent symmetry. You cannot interpret clients' charts without their presence and input, and clients cannot interpret their own charts without the specific knowledge of an astrologer. It is a shared, balanced exchange – rather like a dance – between two human beings.

But before exploring this strange encounter, we first need some background, against which the modern 'astrological consultation' has come into being. The term covers several possible situations, including financial, business or medical astrology, and horary questions about a range of personal topics. In some of these situations the astrologer is expected to offer immediate practical advice, which can then be acted upon by the client, who hopes for a 'yes' or 'no' answer. The aim is to achieve a solution to the problem or question after one session.

My focus, here, is the kind of consultation that might be called a psychotherapeutic exchange. It is more of an inward, reflective journey over a number of sessions. Even if the client arrives with what is known, in psychotherapeutic jargon, as a 'presenting question', the basic difference from the business/horary situation is that the client 'presents' him or herself as a whole person, rather than coming with a question that requires a clear-cut answer. If there is an initial question, it often masks the 'real' issues, which may only surface later, when more inner material has been brought to light.

## A PSYCHOTHERAPEUTIC/PSYCHOANALYTIC MODEL FOR THE ASTROLOGICAL CONSULTATION

However, I'm moving too fast. We need to go back into the nineteenth and twentieth centuries when Sigmund Freud was a catalyst for the psychoanalytic movement, and his 'crown prince', Carl Gustav Jung, developed it along his own distinctive lines. Most of us are familiar with references to Freud's 'talking cure', and to Jung's concept of individuation, and we probably have mental images of what goes on in this type of one-to-one professional encounter.

The figure of the analyst/therapist can be seen in several ways. Imagine a continuum for what might be called 'strict' and 'loose' practice. At one end is the classic picture of the analyst sitting behind the head of the 'patient' (a significant word), lying on a couch. At the other end of the continuum is a more 'New Age' encounter between client and therapist. They are face to face, engaged in role-playing exercises, and they appear to be on a more open and equal footing. The analyst end of the continuum is the 'strict' Freudian model; the New Age end is altogether more relaxed.

Somewhere in the middle, Jungian analysts engage in a structured process: namely to reach the goal of individuation. My own sense is that effective astrological counselling is somewhat nearer to the looser end of therapeutic practice, whilst maintaining clear ethical and professional standards. My reservation about the 'apparent' equality of the looser end is that the issue of a power balance in therapist-client relationships exists in all types of practice. A position of power over the client is not reserved for the often-caricatured figure of the Freudian analyst.

## A 'TYPICAL' ASTROLOGICAL CONSULTATION

There are as many different ways to carry out an astrological consultation as there are individual astrologers practising with clients. It is reasonable, though, to describe the talking-cure exchange as a model. And in addition to professionally qualified astrologers, there are also many unqualified practitioners. So, another continuum could be suggested for the astrological consultation. At the looser end we might have untrained astrologers sitting down to interpret a chart with another person – and often not charging fees – in all kinds of informal settings: around the kitchen table, on the sofa in the family sitting room, across a table in a café or restaurant, or outside in the garden.

At the stricter end are the professional astrologers, who clarify their fees and the length of the session in advance. They may work in a specially designated consulting room, face-to-face or online. After their training, they continue to have personal supervision for their work with clients, and they keep in touch with their peers in the astrological community via astrological organisations, meetings and conferences, and current journals and literature.

In an internet-permeated society, astrologers' contact with each other and with their clients may no longer be face-to-face in the physical sense. I think it's too early to assess the long-term impact of this on the astrological consultation, but the degree of contact astrologers make with their colleagues and the astrological community certainly affects the quality of contact with their clients.

## ASTROLOGICAL CONSULTATION AND 'ORDINARY' THERAPY

So what does the astrological consultation have in common with the talking-cure model? Client and therapist meet for a one-to-one session for an agreed length of time; a fee is paid, and they both hope that the exchange of words will be beneficial. The astrologer appears to be engaged in a similar process to what I am calling the 'ordinary' therapist, but there are also important differences. Like the 'ordinary' encounter, astrological consultations are often an on-going series of meetings; unlike it, on the other hand, a one-off astrological session is not unusual.

In the 1970s, in the early stages of my journey as a consultant astrologer, the one-off session was much more the norm. So, too, were written – rather than face-to-face – consultations. But as an emphasis on counselling skills grew, my practice was growing with it. Later, as tutors in the Faculty, we initiated our Counselling within Astrology training. In addition, I did a three-year 'ordinary' counselling course, and gradually my way of working with clients changed. Of course I understood – from all the training – the need to maintain professional boundaries. And yet, somehow, the unusual dynamic of working together on a birth-chart seemed to make it possible to experience a deep level of emerging friendship, without compromising these boundaries.

My sense is that this may be connected with the length of the gap between sessions. Unlike the regular intervals of 'ordinary' therapy, clients can reappear at very irregular – and sometimes extremely long – intervals. When you first have contact, via a voice at the end of the phone or an e-mail, it's the start of a relationship. I'm still working with people that I've got to know over about thirty years. Some I've seen in a concentrated way – maybe every fortnight, or every month for a while. Some return for annual updates on their chart, and some return at random intervals. And when you get to know somebody over a long period of time, you both change and age, and your relationship develops and deepens.

One thing that has arisen from these erratic time gaps is my long-term practice of writing detailed notes after every session with a client. It's time consuming, but richly rewards the effort involved. Not only do I have a record of the minutiae of our session, but this note-taking also becomes part of the process of supervision. It continues to act as highly personal, inner supervision, in addition to external supervision. When former clients reappear after many years, it makes it possible to carry on as if you'd seen them last week. The 'empty' chart is not enough – that would be like starting all over again with raw symbols. With notes, what you have is context, the client's life and attitudes, and your response to all this. It's tangible clothing for the bare chart.

Having been through hundreds of chart sessions over the last thirty years or so, I have acquired an underground seam of personal material charting my own life path. I suppose I could, at some point, re-read all these notes. They've become a sort of journal, growing out of a professional involvement with other people.

Despite the erratic intervals, the unfolding pattern of astrological progressions and transits creates its own sense of underlying continuity: a sort of coiled rope, which uncoils every time you meet (and meet again and again), prompted by the rhythms of the planets, rather than by the chronological, prescribed intervals of time in 'ordinary' therapy. Even today, however, some astrologers may still decide that they prefer to work on a one-off basis. Ultimately, it's up to the individual client. For whatever reason, many feel that one session (perhaps just in order to have the experience of visiting an astrologer?) is all they want.

However, I now want to explore how the astrological consultation differs from 'ordinary' therapy in a more fundamental way. I think the essential difference is that astrologers work with a birth chart (implying a supernatural or 'other worldly' connection), and that consequently they can represent for their clients what might be called the magician archetype.

## THE MAGICIAN/ASTROLOGER

Whatever astrologers may think is going on in their consultations, it's perhaps more relevant to ask what are the client's perceptions of the process? And this is where the ubiquitous expression 'It's in the stars' is more telling than being a mere cliché. Crucially, it raises the issue of prediction. Some clients will not only perceive the birth-chart as bringing to light certain facets of their character, but also as revealing what the future holds. If astrologers (as 'experts') are able to interpret the chart and therefore to unlock these secrets, then astrologers (as 'magicians') may also be seen as having powers beyond those of an 'ordinary' therapist or counsellor.

And although, in the context of the astrological consultation, I would use the word client rather than patient, the latter term is closer than one might think. Earlier on, I suggested that the power balance in a therapist-

*An Astrologer Casting a Horoscope* (from Robert Fludd's *Utriusque Cosmi Historia*, 1617)

client relationship is a key issue. There are different ways in which it may play out in 'ordinary' therapy, usually – but not always – with the therapist holding the more powerful role. For example, in certain therapeutic disciplines, clients may be told they are 'in denial' if they disagree with the therapist's view.

The astrologer's magician role can represent a very strong power position over the client, and it may seriously distort the balance of the relationship. The 'expert' position is similar to that assigned to analysts, professors, doctors and 'ordinary' therapists. But the cosmic connections can enthral clients in a very different way. Rather than being part of a joint venture – where views are shared and interpretations mutually questioned – the astrologer's client may become a sort of 'patient', i.e. one who submits not only to the one who 'knows better', but also to the one who knows what is 'in the stars' and what lies in the future.

Many years ago, I asked one of my regular clients for permission to use her chart for teaching purposes. To bring the intimate relationship with a client into a public arena – even when it's totally anonymous – has always felt a strange and often uncomfortable process for me. She agreed readily, then exclaimed 'You know all about me! You know my chart!' Her total conviction – expressed with passion – that I had this power shocked me at the time, and still remains with me.

## THE BIRTH CHART AND THE NATURE OF SYMBOL

The other essential difference between the astrological consultation and 'ordinary' therapy or counselling is the presence of the birth-chart. And I am not using the word 'presence' lightly. The chart – the potent container of an intricate pattern of symbols – is far more than a mere reference point or a useful piece of paper that acts as a guide. Does, in fact, the astrological consultation consist of three participants: astrologer, client and chart? In other words, rather than being a one-to-one situation, is it a triangular relationship?

The pattern of astrological symbols within the chart is, quite simply, the heart of the consultation. To engage with it in a transformative way requires the client to possess a symbolic attitude, and without that, s/he may merely be dealing with signs. To summarise the difference between signs and symbols: Signs offer clear directions, probably leading to action or solutions. Symbols are more complex, introspective signs, where subsequent action is not necessarily the aim or outcome – rather they lead to a state of self-knowing.

Both signs and symbols point to something beyond themselves. You could say that every symbol is a sign, but not every sign is a symbol. A sign advises what action to take: for example, a red traffic light tells us to stop. Its function is limited, and it does not invite us to reflect on more profound meanings. A symbol, on the other hand – with its associations flowing out like ripples in a pond – does invite reflection, even meditation. If we took the example of a flower (as a symbol of the ephemeral nature of earthly things) this might conjure up thoughts of life and death, the nature of beauty, growth and decline, and so on. My sense is that, often, clients come to an astrologer looking for signs, and find they are encountering symbols. How they respond to this will depend on whether or not the clients themselves have the symbolic attitude.

If clients, looking for signs, have an urgent question ('Should I move house?') a horary astrologer can provide the 'yes or no' answer they need. If they come to an astrologer offering a psychotherapeutic exchange, they are less likely to be happy with the process.

For example, some years ago, I had a client whose husband's business went into liquidation. This, understandably, left her feeling their secure life was descending into chaos. It happened on the day that transiting Neptune was in exact conjunction with her Capricorn Sun. The beauty and precision of the astrology was a blank for her, as she lacked the symbolic attitude. What she wanted from me was a sign ('This dire situation will soon improve – perhaps next month') rather than a dialogue or reflection on Neptune, a potent symbol. Our perspectives were different; unable to be shared. Whilst I (privately) took delight in that Neptune transit, how could she derive any comfort (if that's the word) from its precision, or – worse still – from discovering that its duration was about two years?

A client's readiness to engage with symbols is the key issue, rather than a specific familiarity with astrological symbols. It is the astrologer's job to translate these, so that the interpretation process becomes a shared experience rather than a 'consultation'. Some clients are keen to learn and to work in this way; some would prefer to steer clear of what they perceive as technical jargon altogether. The astrologer – in any type of consultation – has to make a personal choice whether to involve the client via some degree of translation, or simply to bypass that process and to offer a one-sided interpretation in ordinary everyday language, with minimal reference to the astrological symbols.

But there are so many variables involved. Horary astrologers can work in a poetic and psychological way; business astrologers may choose to involve their clients in the symbolic process, and many literal-minded clients eventually enjoy learning to work with symbols. So – perhaps there are no generalisations to be made? Only, perhaps, to observe that in the course of setting up and developing a practice, it is the real differences between astrologers – in terms of temperament and style of working – that will tend to attract very different kinds of client.

Even after many years of astrological consultations, a phenomenon that never ceases to amaze me is the nervousness, or adrenalin, that surges up before every single meeting with a client. This prior 'space' varies in intensity and discomfort, according to whether I've previously met the client (the worst nervousness is before a first session) and whether they arrive late. It feels like an experience of the Void.

You might think one could fill it with useful tasks, but I've found that impossible. Once waiting, you are 'with' the client in the prospect of being together. For example, a few weeks ago I was seeing a mother and daughter on the same day. Although I knew the mother, I'd never met her daughter, and it was a first session for both of them. Also, I didn't know who was going first (I'd left it up to them to decide) – it was too many unknowns for comfort.

The mother rang to say they were going to be late (when clients do this, it helps, but still leaves an un-fillable space). After about half an hour, I suddenly reached a point of acute edginess. It was bin-collection day in my road, and I suddenly decided to throw out some fish I'd had in the freezer for too long. I reasoned that if it went now, it wouldn't de-compose and smell in the dustbin.

It was at the precise moment I was emerging from the front door, rubber gloves on, carrying this frozen fish to the dustbin (a good Piscean moment…) that my clients appeared. The chart I later set up for this (the consultation chart, I suppose) had some interesting symbolism! This phenomenon may, of course, say more about my personal stuff (with a 'nervy' Uranus rising conjunct the Sun in Gemini) than a general experience for astrologers. Nevertheless, it may be some indication of the strange space into which we venture in every chart session.

## THE PURPOSE OF THE CONSULTATION

What, then, is the purpose of the astrological consultation? Is it to 'heal' or help the client (and/or the astrologer)? Is it to offer some psychological illumination – or is it simply an unusual and creative encounter where healing may or may not occur as a side effect? And does the astrological consultation have anything more to offer than an 'ordinary' therapeutic exchange?

For me, one answer might be what I'd call 'affirmation'. This is when a client leaves at the end of a session (most often a first session) and says s/he feels 'affirmed' by the astrology. And this happens regardless of whether the client has the symbolic attitude, or whether the transits have been difficult. By simply doing your job – interpreting the symbols and interweaving them with the client's nature or situation – you help your clients to feel connected with something supra-personal. They feel they are part of the cosmos, and their life acquires meaning. And to have a sense of meaning is often a definition of the religious attitude.

Another answer might be the depth of relationship that grows in working with somebody for a very long period of time. One of my longest-term clients has been the most difficult I've ever known. In the early years she was extremely demanding, and it required every ounce of patience I possessed to work with her. Once, she rang me on Christmas Day, while I was cooking lunch. But through all the ups and downs, she grew 'into' herself (perhaps as you'd expect with a Sun Capricorn?). Along the way, she gained considerable personal insight, and now our relationship is a joy.

Another 'vintage' client learned the nuts and bolts of astrology. This radically alters the dynamic between astrologer and client. I've had a number of clients who were originally my astrological students, and so we always shared the symbolic language. But to have a 'lay' client who gradually develops into a skilled astrologer has created a rare mutual relationship.

I can't answer for thousands of astrologers, working in their different ways, with a different 'purpose' in mind. But from a personal perspective, I have found that to work with a symbolically-minded client, over a long period of time, is to embark on an extraordinary mutual journey. It can be as profoundly nourishing, on both sides, as are the symbols at the centre of the process. Above all, it is a joint encounter between astrologer, client and chart. I think this triangular relationship, that includes the chart, makes possible a deep friendship between astrologer and client, which is different from the complex ties of transference found in 'ordinary' therapy.

## THE INTERPRETATION TRIANGLE

There needs, however, to be a flowing balance and dialogue between the three participants so that none dominates the encounter. The degree to which the chart is 'allowed' its presence and invited to engage depends on the attitude both of the astrologer and the client. Also, it can depend on where the chart is physically placed. Is it always visible to the client (perhaps on a table between them) or does the astrologer choose to keep it on his or her lap, and out of view, or to work from a computer screen? If clients are relentless talkers, only marginally interested in the chart, and anxious to focus primarily on their own problems in a narrative monologue, then I feel the session becomes closer to 'ordinary' therapy or counselling.

If astrologers are also anxious to hold the stage with their carefully-prepared interpretations (without being interrupted), the session becomes more 'expert dominated'. Clients can feel overwhelmed by all the technical language, and the over-dominant presence of the astrologer, and so experience their own role as passive or secondary. The jargon swamps their need to be 'heard' in everyday language, as human beings rather than a walking chart. Alternatively, it may be the clients themselves who allow the chart to dominate disproportionately, when they defer to it as a sort of oracle, containing magical pronouncements determining their fate and their future.

I am not advocating an 'ideal' balance in the triangle – rather, I'm sketching various scenarios where any of the three participants can take over the prominent position throughout the entire session. If there can be room for all three to listen and talk (client talking, chart talking) then the astrologer's listening skill interweaves the symbols with the client's story, and s/he talks expressively. At its very best, the encounter is a beautiful and creative process, somewhat akin to chamber music or a graceful dance, where each member has a vital contribution to make and no one dominates for too long.

## MARTIN BUBER AND 'I AND THOU'

Finally, I want to mention the philosophy of Martin Buber in relation to the astrological consultation. Buber (1878-1965) was a thinker, philosopher and theologian, and his most famous book – *I and Thou* – was published in 1923. One of his best-known sayings is 'All real living is meeting'[1] and the core of his thought is that the process of relationship lies at the root of meaningful life. This relationship, moreover, is not just restricted to that between one human being and another, but includes encounters with animals, trees, and even stones.

Within this fundamental concept of relationship there are two strands. Buber has two phrases 'I-Thou' and 'I-It' and the difference between the two is basically the difference between a subject-subject relation and a subject-object relation. With I-It, the subject regards the other objectively, as somebody or something he[2] already knows, because they are part of his previous knowledge and experience. In meeting this 'other' he begins to categorise him: to summon up information in order to manage – and to feel in control of – the situation.

With I-Thou, the subject regards the other as another subject, as if he is somebody completely unique. It is as if meeting him is a totally new experience. Buber's lovely phrase for this is 'Its like has not yet been'.[3] They are both together, in the present. In this powerful moment of meeting, the experience is not measured or related to any other previous experience – it simply is what is happening between these two individuals, now. Moreover, it is a reciprocal thing – both subjects are equally present to each other.

Let's take an example. In I-It mode, this subject, meeting me, might describe me as an older woman, English-speaking, with short brown hair and of medium height who lives in London and is a mother, grandmother and an astrologer. In other words, he could define me and put me into a category – and in that sense I'm part of his previous experience (of meeting and summarising people). For him I'm an 'it', and by defining me, he exercises control over his environment, where people can be classified.

However, if we met in I-Thou mode, it would be different. It's not that he would be unaware of the details about me, but, more importantly, he would be with me in that moment: he would be open to me – and I to him – and we would both be alive to how we were reacting to each other as individuals. He would see me as Lindsay, with us in a situation never before experienced, whose like 'has not yet been'.

Similarly, in the context of the astrological consultation, the astrologer in I-It mode might define the client as a 'Libran Sun, with a Capricorn Moon and Ascendant'. In I-Thou mode, s/he would see the client as the embodiment of a unique chart, a whole person.

Buber always points out, though, that one could never be in I-Thou mode all the time – it would be far too highly charged. And he comments that 'The I-Thou relation…is not an unqualified good'.[4] The practical, categorising nature of I-It has its essential place in our lives, just as the astrologer needs the typology of the astrological symbol system as a reference point. The preparation for the session is in I-It mode. The astrologer interacts with the chart; s/he studies its symbols; speculates on possible ways they might be embodied in the client's life; relates these to any previous information from the client, and makes notes. Then the client arrives and is a presence in the room, and the prepared interpretation becomes 'realised'[5] in the act of meeting.

Four years ago, I finished writing a 70,000-word dissertation in which Buber's ideas were the core of my argument. During the extended period of research and writing, I had to reduce my client work substantially. When I returned to a more 'normal' working life, I was curious as to how the experience of reflecting on my own astrological career through concentrated writing would affect my practice. Considering that I was – necessarily – highly articulate during the writing process, I now find it hard to describe the profound change in my work. Perhaps I should be asking those clients who've worked with me 'before and after' if they notice any difference?

Whilst it is far more complex than merely dividing the astrologer's mental processes into left (I-It) and right (I-Thou) brain activity, you might say that – as I suggested – preparing for a session is I-It. The more thoroughly you prepare, the more you are freeing up your mind for I-Thou within the session, when the chart is 'realised' in the living presence of a person. When clients are in front of me, I find I am distracted by checking the dates of transits (the left brain stuff), and less free to focus on the immediacy of their presence.

Post dissertation, another thing I've become more aware of is the curious interchange between emotion and detachment in my work, and perhaps this is another face of I-It/I-Thou? I am detached (I-It) by my intellectual knowledge of the astrological symbol system, yet also emotionally excited when I perceive – sometimes as a sudden, almost Uranian lightning flash – the realisation of a symbol that has sprung into life in that moment. With my earlier example of the client with transiting Neptune conjunct her Capricorn Sun, I felt emotional delight at the symbolism, simultaneously with sadness and empathy (I-Thou) for her distress. That these two states can co-exist is thought-provoking. And if you, and a symbolically-minded client, can be in a mutual state of joy at the manifested symbol, even in the midst of distress, it is truly something extraordinary.

The central core of my thesis was Buber's idea that in meeting another person, one is meeting God. Whereas Buber was a Jewish theologian, astrologers may or may not have any religious attachment. Nevertheless, many feel their work is a spiritual path, and in my writing I deliberately used the phrase 'meeting the divine', rather than 'meeting God'. Whatever one's take on all this, I think the awareness of Buber's ideas has permeated me so that the potential depth of 'meeting' with another person – through client work – can feel like a profound spiritual experience. Not always, but potentially.

## CONCLUSION

At the beginning of this chapter, I suggested that the word 'consultation' implies an asymmetric relationship but that the astrological encounter has an inherent symmetry. I've emphasised that the presence of the birth-chart is the key factor that differentiates an astrological consultation from 'ordinary' counselling or therapy. As a third, active member of the interpretation triangle it relates to the 'other' as a subject – it joins in the dialogue, and brings the flowing energy of the trine aspect into play.

In writing about 'otherness', Buber says 'Genuine conversation...means acceptance of otherness...one accepts and confirms him in his being this particular man made in this particular way.'[6] And he is clear, too, that the subject-subject relation is not merely a question of being warm and friendly to another human being, but must involve *mutuality*:

'He who treats a person as "another I" does not really see that person but only a projected image of himself. Such a relation, despite the warmest "personal" feeling, is really I-It.'[7]

Arguably, I-Thou eventually becomes I-It. But simply to be aware of the two states can sharpen our sense of what goes on between us astrologers, our clients, and our clients' charts. Because this dance can move seamlessly between I-Thou and I-It, we can use typology for clarification, whilst acknowledging the uniqueness of every client: Buber's 'particular man made in this particular way'.

The I-Thou sense of true mutuality – of acknowledging (unique) otherness – makes the astrological encounter an experience of *participation*: an encounter both with our symbols, and with our clients. So in the course of this – and of our journey as 'consultants' – we find that in the realisation of astrological symbols, we begin to *participate* with them. This, and our participation with clients, becomes an embodiment of Martin Buber's *All real living is meeting*.

For us as astrological consultants, to bring clients into the discovery that the symbols in their charts are living entities, rather than dead glyphs on a piece of paper, can be the most satisfying, and ultimately awe-inspiring, way of working as an astrologer. And then – if our clients are able to enjoy a mutual and equal sense of participation – it becomes an extraordinary journey, with the 'astrological consultation' as a place of true meeting. For me, it is qualitatively different from any other sort of therapeutic practice.

### NOTES

1. Martin Buber and Ronald G. Smith, *I and Thou*, 2nd rev. edn (New York: Scribner, 1958), p.25.

2. I am choosing to use the masculine pronoun throughout this description, in deference to Buber's own usage in his writing.

3. Martin Buber and Ronald G. Smith, *Between Man and Man* (London: Kegan Paul 1947), pp.16-17.

4. Maurice S. Friedman, *Martin Buber: The Life of Dialogue* (London: Routledge and Kegan Paul, 1955) [hereafter *Martin Buber: The Life of Dialogue*], p.60.

5. I am using the terms 'speculative' and 'realised' interpretation in the sense originated by Geoffrey Cornelius. For a discussion of this see Geoffrey Cornelius, *The Moment of Astrology: Origins in Divination*, rev. edn (Bournemouth: Wessex Astrologer, 2003), pp. 292-296.

6. *Martin Buber: The Life of Dialogue*, p.82.

7. *Martin Buber: The Life of Dialogue*, p.61.

Chapter Seven
# LIVING AN ASTROLOGICAL PHILOSOPHY: ASTROLOGY AS GUIDE AND SPIRITUAL PRACTICE
## DIANE CONWAY

There is a long history of describing astrology as a means of navigation. The journey of life becomes, by analogy, a voyage on the high seas and our beginnings are watery enough, twisting and rocking at anchor in the amniotic fluid of the home port, with the Ascendant gaining a flavour of the harbour wall, as well as the degree rising above the eastern horizon at the time and place of birth, or embarkation. For Hellenistic astrologers the first house was amongst other things the helm and the chart ruler the helmsman, or steersman who guided the ship to its destination.[1]

A seafaring voyage may employ charts and draw up maps of the journey travelled, with markers. Popularly, astrology bears the tempting lure of 'telling the future', like the flash of a tart's lacy garter, but we do not need to have journeyed all that far to know the powerful role of the beginning of a tale in determining its ending and particularly the form in which the past is charted and the mental furniture with which it is marked and the style in which it continues to be re-told.

The first thing I wanted to be was a poet. Aged seven, the love of words, the unchartered waters they could plumb and their symbolic configurations could imply, coalesced into a marker, something I wanted to be, like a stone could be plucked from beneath a breaking wave and held in the hand and embody the ocean in the way the sunlight caught the seawater on its surface and exploded the kaleidoscope of crystalline colours. Then it dried and became a stone again and I saw the Mystery somewhere else. I made a little cairn of such stones in the garden.

Somewhat in this spirit, in navigating the ground in this chapter I will be using literature as a reference point to assist unpacking the area I will be exploring – three favourite poems and a children's classic form the four points of the compass because I am who I am. I have a fascination in using words to draw meaning from symbols – a preoccupation shared by astrologers and poets – and these pieces are part of my life, just as astrology has been for upwards of twenty years or more, and speak to me.

## DISPLACED ART

I remember the hush that fell over the room when Vicki Feaver read this poem[2] on a workshop, she the poet, me the pupil, rather a precocious pupil in that I was then in my mid-teens. She suggests the fact that she has no space for writing her poetry – no room of her own, no specific desk even – has wider and deeper resonance and is symbolic of the way her art and calling is treated by society.

When we fell into general discussion later, the question: what did I want to do with my life? But you can't do this, this is not a profession… or hardly ever. I have had this conversation on several occasions, firstly poetry, but not least about astrology. This was clearly a voyage off the map. Maps no longer have gods and goddesses in the margins with tridents, strange composite beasts. The modern world does not value symbols. Grains of sand no longer have worlds inside, they are useful building materials. Stones are stones.

Would it have helped if someone had said, or more loudly, this is first and foremost a spiritual practice – monks chant, dervishes whirl, you do this or – even if you don't do this, it will haunt you, you will get more pleasure from doing this than from – almost – anything. It is love in motion. If you don't do this, you won't feel truly alive but yes, of course, you need to live and earn and keep a roof over your head and pay your taxes, just like everyone else – this may, or may not help you to do that – and everyone else choruses that they have such busy lives, with never time to fit it all in. You have all that – and this.

Developing one's astrological craft can be wisely approached as a spiritual practice.

Spiritual practice is practice. It takes time and nerve and effort. There is never enough time but, with tenacity and focus, much can be accomplished. If you wait for the right time, you could wait a lifetime and miss an opportunity. It is surprising what can be carved out of the tail end of a day, or a dawn, like Napoleonic prisoners whittled schooners out of old bones that would otherwise be buried or wasted. It requires persistence and regular commitment, a little bit here, a little bit there. You have to carefully consider your priorities. There is a lot to learn, more to put into practice, even more to read.

Gradually, may you grow. May mini epiphanies light your path, if you persist. May chart factors that were dead notes learn to speak. May intractable T-squares still shriek their old songs but learn some harmonies, to save you all from going entirely mad. May family and friends learn to become more tolerant, even if they never entirely understand. May you find precious friends who speak the language.

It may never entirely make sense from a worldly point of view but, in a world that seems to favour triviality and conformity, we can create our room of our own, whether literal or metaphorical, an alchemical place, tend a sacred flame that has been passed down to us quietly, between the cupped hands of our teachers, who have received it from their teachers, in due time pass it on.

We may eventually learn to respect, maybe even to love, the areas of loneliness, of hunger, of non-conformity, of alienation that give us the space to continue to do so.

Against expectation, perhaps, it does not give up quietly, or give in: marginalised, yet persistent. Vikki Feaver gives a haunting picture of her art and her calling.

Wandering on like the itinerant Fool in the tarot, with his pack on his back, always looking back, we are told – whether warily, or reflectively, we are left to ponder – is it merely shiftless, driven by its inner demons, or the initiate's gnosis, misunderstood by the world, carrying subversive wisdom to its next safe liberal haven?

I am mindful also of the travels of astrology itself, midnight flits from Babylon, to Alexandria, to Athens, to Rome, to Harran, Baghdad, Florence, stashed in a ship's hold, or a camel's saddlebag, watchful, unobtrusive, keeping one step ahead of burning. Vicki Feaver speaks of her art as a 'defiant weed'. True to the spirit of the old gardener's adage that a weed is a flower in the wrong place, maybe we can offer a safe haven for weeds and a prayer of thanks that we are in a position to offer such.

Wily and fated to wander, astrology travels on.

We may throw our lot in with astrology and travel alongside, sharing our experiences but, even if we fall out and cease communication, stare unseeingly at the wall as in a tube train carriage, we still remain ship mates.

The legends say an oracle warned Odysseus that, if he set sail for Troy, he would not return for twenty years and then alone and penniless. 'He therefore feigned madness'...[3]

*Odysseus Departs from the Land of the Phaecians* (Claude Lorrain, 1646)

# LIVING AN ASTROLOGICAL PHILOSOPHY

## ITHAKA

> 'As you set out for Ithaka
> hope your road is a long one,
> full of adventure, full of discovery'.[4]

Nothing remains on a long voyage but sea and sky; we head for the horizon, (from which our journey began, astrologically speaking at the Ascendant) and at night, the stars come out and become the clearest thing, we plot our course by them, we navigate and, on a long watch, ponder if the old tales of their qualities are true but, even so, we do not expect to reach them, even the few who have heard whispers of the old magicians' tales of the Ship of Solomon.

Astrology is a journey and not a destination.

Whether we have a sense of meeting, or renewing an old acquaintance, whether it is a slow smouldering attraction or love at first sight, the all-consuming fixation of a passionate affair, we encounter astrology but it is not something we can ever entirely learn, or encompass, or possess – like the abstraction of the horizon it is always in sight, almost within grasp, but leading us on.

A course, a workshop, a book, an interpretation may give an artificial sense of potential finitude and accomplishment, yet what we reach out to possess eludes us, runs like water between our hands. Profound distress can spring from this. Exercises wind on, labyrinthine, haunt our dreams, deadlines and study plans melt and distort like Dali's clocks. All may go swimmingly until Life Intervenes, in a big way sometimes.

It is as if a lever marked 'Astrology' triggers Pandora's box although, Astrology, like Hope, lingers on to help us pick our way through the wreckage of our lives, assigning significance, we can train our ears to the particular reverberations structures make as they fall, gaining a visceral sense of the feel of a transit, the synchronicities illuminate our inner sky like the Blitz illuminated London.

Whilst Astrology lights her cigarette and whispers that if, like moths to a flame, we, her lovers, burn and she remains blameless, we may question that, feel scarred by the accelerated process of derma-peel she seems to activate in our soul as she transforms and renews us.

As within, so without; the Laestrygonians, Cyclops, angry Poseidon – the poet C.P. Cavafy suggests we have no reason to fear the grotesque monsters and angry gods that attempt to thwart and delay our safe passage as, if we did not bring them with us, within our souls, we would not encounter them.

The Lady Astrology evokes courage and honesty in her lovers and, as I have mentioned before, persistence.

After a while, wearily we set down our firefighting equipment and feel we may now dust down our astrology bag and journey further.

'Hope your road is a long one'... Whilst, at times, the relief of knowing when a particular transit ends is undeniable, in broader terms the ceaseless whining of the inner child repeating 'Are we nearly there yet?' has surely missed the point. Where is there? Leafing through the ephemeris, faster and faster, looking vainly for relief, for stasis, transit follows transit, it is as if we are Alice in Wonderland, or through the Looking Glass, fighting a pack of cards, whilst simultaneously we unfold slowly, inexorably by progression like the slow motion film of the blooming of a flower. A quiet, soulful voice murmurs death is journey's end and, if arguably (as phrased so memorably by Joe Landwehr), from the point of view of Spirit: 'death is but a speed bump on the road to eternal life'[5] from the ensouled and embodied point of view, that is surely no way to enjoy a holiday.

Ithaka, Ithaka, always heading to Ithaka, how much is our destination our destiny? We are adjured by Cavafy to hasten slowly, to trust the process, to fill our bellies, to savour the moment, as the accumulated experience is the true wealth we bring. Ithaka itself seems poor in comparison. It is a spiritual hunger, the tide that carries us.

Living, working, loving, sleeping alongside astrology, an awareness of rhythm develops, a trust in the process, half-waking, amongst the dreams or the night terrors, astrology lies softly nearby like a long-time lover. As honesty develops self-awareness and a steady acceptance of one's power it becomes slowly apparent that one has fallen in love with oneself in the mirror, as ever, recognising shining brightly in another the potential that glows but dimly in ourselves. Through work, through time, through love, pain, forgiveness, self-acceptance, we become the wealth, the fullness, the experience we seek, what was out there is now in here and what difference is there – in truth. When journey's end arrives we will embrace Ithaka and astrology, like an ancestral ghost greeting us.

This will be another port to explore and Cavafy evokes richly the joy of continued discovery, the foreign sights, smells and sensations, the exotic riches of the markets at each successive harbour, each city offering the exciting opportunities 'to learn and go on learning from their scholars'[6]. Hanging on to their words, talking late into the night, into the small hours until the dew rises cool on the grass around you, no wonder the journey is so long, but who would cut short such pleasure by a single day? The sense of discovery and impending wonder is so strong, fresh as salt on the wind, the space, the newness, the potential beyond the horizon, beckoning, assails you.

## ON FIRST LOOKING INTO CHAPMAN'S HOMER

'Then felt I like some watcher of the skies
When a new planet swims into his ken;'[7]

Blind Homer strums his lyre and sings of the fall of Troy and the wanderings of Odysseus (Keats heard him and wrote a sonnet) and we still listen, even after thousands of years; perhaps his very blindness heightens poetry's magic, the power of rediscovery and of seeing afresh. It is the magic of the inspired use of symbol, how one thing can illuminate another, it is the skilled eye that knows where to facet the diamond, the patient watcher who discerns the planet from the star. Yes, Keats heard him and had a vision, in a manner of speaking.

We are told Keats was then aged twenty and a medical student. He spent a night drinking and talking poetry, taking turns to recite aloud from Chapman's verse translation of Homer's *Iliad* which tells of the fall of Troy. Richard Holmes describes the night in detail in *The Age of Wonder* where he explores how voyages of scientific discovery made around the turn of the 18th century acted as inspiration for the contemporary Romantic poets. He reminds us how the meeting place of art and science, of right and left brain can be a potent place.

We are told very early the next morning, in 1816, Keats wrote a sonnet called *On First Looking into Chapman's Homer* celebrating how, through Homer, he had seen the world anew, afresh, expanded – like the great explorer, Cortez, or the great astronomer, Herschel, discovering Uranus.

As above, so below – everything is interconnected and in a state of intercommunication.

Looking at the discovery, the poem, Richard Holmes' beautiful exposition, through astrological eyes, we very likely have first-hand knowledge of what it feels like to experience such a 'metaphysical shift' and 'moment of revelation'[8] when science and art come together. The sudden rush of unbounded vision, for a split second before it fades, the glimpses of the infinite are surely amongst the peak moments that makes astrology so addictive. We do not have to be singular to experience this, in terms of being a historically noteworthy figure – whether astronomer, explorer, or poet – merely to be singular in terms of allowing our life to be guided by what is widely regarded as an outmoded cosmology and system of thought, which has been allowed to roll to the periphery from the centre, like a ruby in the dust.

By observing inter-reflections, by use of simile, by bringing different subjects and specialisms into dialogue, revelations are born, intellectual understanding is expanded, emotional understanding is enhanced, spiritual growth is made; astrology is now and for several centuries has been popularly excluded from this debate, made to stand alone, like an idiot, in the corner. At one time astrology enriched libraries, academies, symposia – now no longer, largely. Libraries burnt, scholars fled, ancient academies empty and derelict, doors swinging, open to the stars in a more literal fashion. Astrology survived like a precious painting rent free from its frame and carried off to safety whilst the frame and the palace burned. Survived out of context, often in partial concealment, many volumes lost, consigned to the flames, or lying untranslated.

The first line of attack in an attempt at mass subjugation of a group is to: 'erase the traces of its memory in order to reconfigure its identity'[9]. Fernando Baez describes how, as symbols of collective memory, of the collected works of the feared and hated opposition, books are burned and libraries bombed, arguments are annihilated symbolically by the act of bibliocaust. Books are attacked not for what they are, but for what they represent. Reason itself is torched by a flaming inferno which: 'reduces the spirit of a work to matter.... That which is light becomes dark'.[10]

Baez' work in *A Universal History of the Destruction of Books* evokes the sense of a perpetually rolling sea where storms of clashing ideologies ferment, where tides of scholarship are endlessly overtaken by waves of destruction, repeatedly, throughout history. Arguably, in the face of this storm, we, as astrologers, like

*The Great Library of Alexandria* (Otto von Corvin)

beachcombers may be inspired to make practical use of what remains of our tradition, the random flotsam disgorged by the sea which is available, to hand, while times allow: to nourish it, to cherish it as it stands but also perhaps to attempt in whatever individual way we can to weave it back into the fabric of wider intellectual study from which it has been torn, to release it from the confines of its esoteric ghetto, to expand both our vision and wider intellectual debate by seeing how it fits in with everything else. To invest our time, skill, dedication in this task and to make it another strand of our spiritual practice.

We are personally responsible for the survival of our tradition. 'We all stand as links in a chain of transmission which must not be allowed to fail.'[11]

Our prospective journey is vast and yet strangely familiar, John and Caitlin Matthews tell us.

We all have our passions and specialisms outside astrology with which astrology can dialogue, potentials for intellectual cross-pollination and evolution which may enrich. Equally, we are in a position to respond to new developments. We are children of our age. We can see, looking back, astrology has been a motley, harlequin tradition, syncretic, blending elements of Babylon, Egypt, Greece, expanding in harmony with a slowly expanding universe and discovery and perception of such and this process appears ongoing and eternal.

For receptive minds, the dizzying immensity of the night sky is deeply inspiring, its role as an inerasable repository of myth, giving intimations of eternity and the existence of other realities and other worlds, gently corroborating the seeds dropped by half-forgotten tales told long ago. Like a picture within a painting, C. S. Lewis' *Prince Caspian* played this role in my life.

## NARNIA

'And there never was a time when animals could talk. Do you hear?'[12]

The children's classic *Prince Caspian* is one of C. S. Lewis' seven chronicles of Narnia. In this volume, as in many of the series, by various magical means, human children find themselves moving into a different world where they become Kings and Queens and where time appears to move at a different speed. In each case, the time when the two worlds and time frames intersect proves pivotal and significant, for both the children and for Narnia. The fact that two time frames might conceivably intersect meaningfully should not surprise us; we know how a day and a year may equate symbolically by secondary progression, for example. However, in Narnia stars can be conversed with face to face as they await their heliacal rising. When one of the more scientifically-minded human children asserts that, in our world, a star would be seen as a flaming ball of gas he is countered:

'Even in your world, my son, that is not what a star is but only what it is made of.'[13]

It is unclear how much Narnia is to be viewed as a different world, or a different dimension of our own world which is more actively ensouled and awake. This dimension can be silenced by a materialistic outlook, or awakened by active engagement with image and with symbol; what is awakened is not only another dimension in the world, but in ourselves. *Prince Caspian* gives an account of this process unfolding. As astrologers, we should not be surprised to find ourselves in Narnia, in the land of the Fauns, Centaurs and talking beasts, where the River God raises his head to speak, where the Dryads animate the trees to pour down the hill in pursuit of their oppressors and feast on choicest loam after their victory. Just like the children magic-ed to Narnia, two worlds collide when we encounter astrology. As the faerie is wont to say in the fairy tale: 'Which eye did you see me with?' We are transported from the modern day to a strange and ancient land.

Sadly, it is perhaps no accident that *Prince Caspian* was promoted primarily as a children's book as – despite countless millennia of experience to the contrary – looking through the eye of modern consensus reality, we are the only centre of consciousness and meaning in a dead universe of raw materials and to suggest otherwise is to see through the eye of our projections in a way that is lamentably self-indulgent and childish. Richard Tarnas gives a detailed exploration of this philosophical position and its implications for astrology in Cosmos and Psyche.[14]

The Narnia to which the children are summoned in *Prince Caspian* is under the rule of a usurper, Miraz. The Naiads and Dryads have been silenced, the Dwarfs, Fauns, Centaurs, talking beasts live in fear and in hiding; the children assist in the reanimation of that world and the restoration of Old Narnia under the rulership of the true king, the young Prince Caspian but, when the tale begins, the only glimpses of that world afforded to Caspian are the treasured bedtime stories of his nurse, the most precious hour of the day in the grand, but lonely life he lives in his uncle's castle.

King Miraz says, as he and his wife are childless, the orphaned Caspian will as likely succeed him and be King himself one day and, what more could he wish for? Caspian's innocent wish that he lived in the Old Days and his babbled depiction of Old Narnia provokes a sharp and thunderous response. Miraz wants to know what he has heard and from whom he has heard it but in no uncertain terms makes it clear such is childish rubbish and he never wants to hear the like again. Like any sensitive child who has premonitions, or says he sees ghosts, or fairies, or angels, Caspian grows up very quickly when he shares Nurse's tales of talking beasts and spiritual beings, Naiads and Dryads, Dwarfs and Fauns.

Nurse is summarily banished and replaced by a tutor, Doctor Cornelius, fairy tales are replaced by history, but, as he matures, Caspian continues to follow the same thread.

'Perhaps it is time to turn from History to Grammar'[15] but Caspian resists. He pleads and protests to Doctor Cornelius; a matter of history arrests and troubles him. Why was his ancestor called Caspian the Conqueror if there was nobody in Narnia to fight with him? His tutor repeats pointedly and enigmatically that, at the time of the conquest, there were few men in Narnia.

'For a moment Caspian was puzzled and then suddenly his heart gave a leap. "Do you mean," he gasped, "that there were other things? Do you mean it was like in the stories? Was there – ?"'[16]

Mesmeric fireside tales of the old days have morphed into seditious theories but remain intellectual abstractions. The Doctor warns caution. These are dangerous secrets, not to be repeated. If they reached the King's ears, Caspian would be whipped and the doctor should have his head cut off.

Why do we return to certain tales and hold them close to our heart? Favourite children's stories are a little read oracle but can be worthy of further study. Astrology can be consigned to a ghetto inside ourselves as well as in wider intellectual debate; we may 'believe' in things but do not admit we do. Consensus reality can be very persuasive. For years, *Prince Caspian* provided quiet words of caution and reassurance. However, returning to the book again to write this, I am struck afresh how powerfully it centres and turns on an astrological initiation.

Doctor Cornelius announces he is to give Caspian an astronomy lesson. It seems a pleasant distraction, at first, to Caspian, of no particular relevance to his life, or to his growing fascination with Old Narnia. At dead of night, two planets, Tarva and Alambil will be in close conjunction, within one degree, for the first time in two hundred years, for the only time in a lifetime.

When he is awoken, the room is full of moonlight. He and the Doctor are to wear hooded robes and soundless slippers. They pass through passages, locked doors, empty chambers, climb several staircases, up onto the leads of the castle roof and thence to the central tower where Caspian has never previously been allowed access.

He sees the battlements and roofs below him, patchworked with shadows and shimmering with moonlight, the gardens beyond, the gleam of a distant river whose waterfall breaks the intense and expectant silence, the outline of far mountains.

He sees the two stars he has come to see, bright as little moons and very close together.

So far it has been an interesting diversion, with curiosity value only, to get up in the night, to dress in strange robes, but, with the conjunction in sight, the atmosphere changes, the tension mounts, the language becomes subtly more powerful and archaic. This is a once in a lifetime moment; the intellectual perception of this, the active acknowledgment of it, combined with the conscious participation and engagement in it and with it, allows the gulf between earth and sky to be breached, like lightning strike, the two worlds to become one and both to be changed, with the participants to be the active conductors of the new energy.

Doctor Cornelius has a further hidden agenda. He agrees they would have seen the conjunction better from a different tower. He brought Caspian here for another reason. The reason is the isolation of the spot. Caspian is sworn to secrecy and told the truth, which brings new responsibility. It is his race that silenced the beings of Old Narnia and is now attempting to erase even the memory of them. It soon transpires that, on the birth of a son of his own, Miraz is to attempt to obliterate even Caspian.

Whatever confused perceptions we hold, for whatever reason confused, we may navigate by the stars, who do not forget the steps of their dance, however complex, however long and thus the truth unfolds like a tangled rope; it may unravel with surprising speed once set in motion, by active involvement with astrological symbolism when the time is ripe, a powerful astrodrama, or guided meditation, by participation in ritual work, a well-timed initiation. The truth, we are told, sets us free. We are marked by the occasion in our own way like lightning-blasted oaks, the figurehead of our own revolution, just as Caspian becomes the willing figurehead for the liberation of Old Narnia and is recognised as such by the Centaur,

Glenstorm. A prophet and star-gazer, he is first to hail Caspian confidently as King and to call for open battle to drive Miraz out of Narnia. Nobody else had ever dreamed of more than guerrilla raids, although Caspian is armed and armoured.

"'The time is ripe," said Glenstorm. "I watch the skies... for it is mine to watch, as it is yours to remember. Tarva and Alambil have met in the halls of high heaven..."'[17]

May you journey well. May you unfold whatever gift lies within you and become more than you ever imagined possible.

### NOTES

1. Demetra George, *Astrology and the Authentic Self: Integrating Traditional and Modern Astrology to Uncover the Essence of the Birth Chart* (Lake Worth, FO: Ibis Press, 2008), pp.85-86.

2. Vicki Feaver, *Displaced Art* from *Close Relatives: Poems* (London: Martin Secker and Warburg Limited, 1981), p.32.

3. Robert Graves, *The Greek Myths* (Middlesex: Folio Society Edition, 1998), p.581.

4. C.P. Cavafy, Ithaka from C.P. Cavafy *Collected Poems*, trans. by Edmund Keeley and Philip Sherrard (London: Chatto and Windus Limited, 1978) [hereafter *Ithaka*], p.29.

5. Joe Landwehr, *The Seven Gates of Soul: Reclaiming the Poetry of Everyday Life* (St. Louis, MO: Ancient Tower Press, 2004), p. 33.

6. *Ithaka*, p.29.

7. John Keats, *On First Looking into Chapman's Homer* anthologised in *Poems on the Underground: Fifth Edition*, ed. by Gerard Benson, Judith Chernaik and Cicely Herbert (London: Cassell Publishers Limited, 1995), p.96.

8. Richard Holmes, *The Age of Wonder: How the Romantic Generation Discovered the Beauty and Terror of Science* (London. Harper Press, 2009), p.207.

9. Fernando Baez, *A Universal History of the Destruction of Books: From Ancient Sumer to Modern Iraq* trans. from the Spanish by Alfred MacAdam (London: Atlas and Co, 2008) [hereafter *A Universal History*], p.12.

10. *A Universal History*, p.17.

11. Caitlin and John Matthews, *The Western Way: A Practical guide to the Western Mystery Tradition* (London: Arkana, 1994), p.427.

12. C.S. Lewis, *Prince Caspian – The Return to Narnia* (London: Puffin Books, 1962) [hereafter *Prince Caspian*], p.44.

13. C.S. Lewis, *The Voyage of the Dawn Treader* (London: Puffin Books, 1965), p.177.

14. Richard Tarnas, *Cosmos and Psyche: Intimations of a New World View* (London: New York: Viking Penguin, 2006), pp.18-19.

15. *Prince Caspian*, p.46.

16. *Prince Caspian*, p.46.

17. *Prince Caspian*, p.72.

Chapter Eight

# ASTROLOGY IN THE MODERN WORLD

## LAURA ANDRIKOPOULOS

Modern men and women seem to have forgotten the enchanting possibility of their souls being connected to the stars. More fundamentally, many have forgotten they have a soul at all. Thus does the budding astrologer awaken to a world in which he or she is somewhat out of place, a person on the fringes of society; an outcast in an era of secular modernity that makes a radical distinction between psyche and cosmos and struggles to contemplate any possible connection between the two.

This stage of the journey through astrology is potentially one of disillusionment, dissatisfaction, and despair, followed by a period of intense reflection leading to reconciliation of a Chironian kind. One accepts that an astrologer in the modern world may always be somewhat at odds with mainstream society and therefore that astrologers carry a wound that will never heal. Acceptance of the wound allows the individual touched by astrology to relate to modern Western culture in full awareness of their predicament, and to choose their ongoing path in the knowledge they are unlikely to ever fully integrate two colliding worldviews.

I always remember having an interest in astrology, although I could not tell you where or how this first arose. As a teenager I would occasionally buy books connected with the subject, although I realise now that these were books very far from the more serious end of the market. They whetted my appetite however for a subject deliciously different from the more usual offerings. I had always felt a strong inner sense of destiny, so anything that spoke to that intuition appealed greatly. I never doubted for a second that

I had a soul, but the more educated I became the more I realised this was often considered a strange belief to hold in the modern world. Finding astrology helped embody soul within cosmos and provided a framework for the meaning that seemed so clearly a part of human life, but it also opened up a gulf between my own understanding of the world and that of many people around me.

## TO BE MODERN IS TO BE SEPARATE

The citizen of the modern Western world is a separate individual. With the advent of the mechanistic philosophy during the scientific revolution, human beings of the Western cultural tradition lost their sense of participating in an animate cosmos, instead learning to perceive the world around them as a separate, detached, and lifeless thing. The world was something to be observed without individual involvement, and the more objectivity, the better. The very basis of the scientific worldview, as Thomas Nagel has so aptly suggested, is the 'view from nowhere'[1]. The individual and their unique subjective relationship with the cosmos is an irrelevant factor.

No wonder then that astrology is so painfully out of sync with the times. Science and technology are the gods of our age and anything connected with meaning, soul, and individual mystical experience is seen as inferior and often regarded with deep scepticism. Whilst both religion and astrology face this problem, the great difficulty for astrology is that it has often been seen as a form of primitive science, a way of understanding the causal structure of the world that has clearly been superseded by the scientific advances of the day. Not only then is astrology rejected knowledge on the basis of its affinity with meaning and soul, but also because it is seen as an absurd upstart to the sophisticated and properly scientific theories currently in vogue. It is neither science nor religion, and thus in the stark categories of modern knowledge struggles to find a home.

## THE PARADOX OF MODERN FREEDOM

Yet it is not only classification problems that lead to astrology's rejection as a respectable practice or form of knowledge in the modern West. Astrology is often seen as an affront to that most precious, albeit paradoxical in the light of scientific determinism, idea of the freedom of the modern person.

The modern person is alienated from the cosmos, and therefore faces life in existential angst; one of the great burdens of modernity being the freedom to choose. Freedom brings responsibility; if I choose X, I exclude Y and Z; if I do nothing, I still choose – I become a passive spectator as the world passes me by. Yet this perceived freedom, despite it being a heavy burden, is valued deeply by modern Western consciousness; it is enshrined in our laws and democracies. It is a fundamental aspect of the great value placed on the individual human person in liberal Western society.

The path that astrology walks between freedom and fate is a tenuous one. Whilst the vast majority of modern astrologers would not hold to any full astral determinism, they would often accept a state of affairs whereby the individual is constrained by the archetypal pattern of their own nature, and the inherent timing of the unfolding of that pattern.

Properly applied, this astro-cosmology could be used to increase an individual's freedom. The greater awareness an individual has of his or her own nature, the easier it is to be free since one is able to choose and act in full awareness of one's own inclinations and inner conflicts. Unfortunately, as we will explore further below, the two dominant faces of astrology in modernity do not allow for such a subtle position to be understood by the average person. Astrology in its most populist, fortune-telling guise, and also in its poorly understood 'serious' form, become an affront to the liberated individual. It is then discarded by those who find its potential for stereotyping, passivity and fatalism incompatible with decent 21st century living.

My experiences of astrology were not always positive. I have always remembered receiving a computerised report supposedly summarising some of the main features of my birth-chart. One section had particularly stuck out, as it had stated that when young all of my relationships with the opposite sex would be unfulfilling, as I would struggle to reconcile the physical and emotional aspects of the partnership. This felt like a curse, a bind that I could not avoid and which, even if true, I would rather not have known about. As a young woman, the last thing I wanted to be told was that all my relationships for the next fifteen years were going to be unsatisfying! Later, I understood where this comment had come from – an opposition in my birth-chart between the planets Mars and Venus – but it still angers me

# ASTROLOGY IN THE MODERN WORLD

*Soul in Bondage* (Elihu Vedder, 1891-2)

that someone had thought it appropriate to word their interpretation in so definite a fashion, with no helpful advice as to how to manage the conflict, or even encouragement that the conflict could indeed be managed.

Thus was I early alerted to some of the dangers of astrology and its clash with one of the enshrined principles of contemporary Western life; our freedom to create the lives we wish and our ability to be autonomous and self-determining. Yet I was not put off. A few years later, having just come out of a difficult relationship, I found myself landed on the website of the Faculty of Astrological Studies. Little did I realise the import of the journey that was about to begin.

This then was when I really discovered astrology, for through the Faculty I encountered astrology presented in serious, ethical form. I found a course that was written by intelligent, sensitive people, understanding the need to tread carefully around making interpretations about other human beings, yet also managing to communicate the magic, depth and wonder of a truly fascinating subject.

I was immediately hooked. I knew I had discovered something of immense importance, which could reveal profound matters and shed light on that sense of destiny which deep down still resonated. So I studied for and gained my Diploma, all the time reading avidly and doing chart after chart for almost everyone I knew and met. At the same time however, I kept one foot firmly in the other world, the modern, sensible but dull world, holding down a full-time job in a respectable profession and purchasing my first home.

The astrological fever lasted many years. I immersed myself in the subject. I became involved in the running of the Faculty, eventually being elected President. I tutored astrological students, saw clients and eventually, after the birth of my second child, drifted away from mainstream employment so that all my work interests now revolved around astrology. Astrology was a joyful, thrilling adventure, allowing one to see the world through imaginal eyes, bringing the lifeless modern world back to glory and colour. The starkness of the contrast however revealed a problem yet to be fully faced.

## THE DOMINANT FACES OF ASTROLOGY IN MODERNITY

The aspiring astrologer faces the task of coming to terms with the two dominant faces of astrology in current Western consciousness.

The first is an astrology of trivia; of Sun-sign columns and phone lines attached to newspapers and magazines that allude to great things but provide only the most general intimation of the complex edifice that lies beneath the 'signs' and twelve-fold daily interpretations. This mass, or pop astrology, as the corporate lawyers are careful to point out, is strictly 'for entertainment only' and therefore does not have to be taken seriously by anyone with any level of intelligence. It is just 'a bit of fun', an unimportant and rather silly distraction from the scientific rigour and technological innovation of modern life.

The second face recognises that there are some people (unbelievably) who take astrology seriously in our modern Western world. Such persons are regarded suspiciously and often characterised as the sort of people who reject the advances of modern science and instead believe that all human life is determined by planetary movements in direct, causal fashion. These laughable holders of fringe beliefs are periodically denounced by those respectable persons known to have some scientific credentials, but who for the most part have very little understanding or knowledge of what the contemporary astrologer actually does or believes.

## MODERNISING REFORM WITHIN ASTROLOGY

Astrologers have not been immune to the challenges facing their subject in modernity. Throughout the 20th century in particular, reforming zeal and a modernising spirit has characterised the work of the major astrological writers.

The first reformer of note was the theosophist, Alan Leo (1860-1917), who dedicated himself to reforming astrology and integrating it with the doctrines of karma and reincarnation, which were central to his own philosophy of life. He simplified techniques, and expanded character description through long analysis of zodiac signs, thereby paving the way for later and more thorough psychologisation of the subject. Leo's mantra was 'character is destiny' and following several brushes with the fortune-telling laws of his day, he stepped up his campaign to rid astrology of fated predictions. Character delineation was the sort of astrology fit for modernity.

The second great reformer of modern Western astrology was the French-American Dane Rudhyar (1895-1985), also a theosophist, but perhaps more importantly, someone inspired by the early work of the psychologist Carl Gustav Jung (1875-1961). Rudhyar's ground-breaking work was his first book, *The Astrology of Personality*, published in 1936, in which he endeavoured to place astrology in the context of modern thought, particularly through its compatibility with modern psychology.[2]

As Rudhyar was quick to identify, Jung's work was particularly applicable to astrology. At the time, this may have seemed a most fortuitous connection, and as if astrology was on the brink of some form of scientific acceptance, it seeming to dovetail so neatly with the theories of one of the major psychological thinkers of the age. This was not however a remarkable coincidence, nor an example of one of Jung's signature concepts, synchronicity.

Jung was steeped in the esoteric traditions and mythologies of the past, and related his own work in psychology to Gnosticism and alchemy. He was interested in astrology from as early as 1911 until his death in 1961, and it is likely that astrological ideas, along with other esoteric traditions and sources, influenced at least some of his major concepts. Whilst this does not take away his importance as a major thinker whose work shows great overlap with certain currents in modern astrology, he cannot be called upon as an independent verifier of the ancient art itself.

Despite this, the project to fuse Jungian psychology and astrology remained a major theme of late 20th century astrology. This reached its peak in the work of Liz Greene (1946- ), a Jungian analyst and astrologer whose prolific written output includes around twenty books of psychological astrology, which contain sophisticated interweaving of various psychological concepts with natal horoscopes, drawing heavily on Jungian ideas. Other notable psychological astrologers of the period include Stephen Arroyo (1946- ), Howard Sasportas (1948-1992), and Karen Hamaker-Zondag (1952- ).

Individuation stands out as a particularly important Jungian concept for such astrologers. This is the idea that each individual is on a path to growth involving gradual assimilation of the unconscious part of their psyche into the conscious part. This path to wholeness and philosophy of psychological awareness forms a background to the majority of serious astrological texts in the second half of the 20th century. In such texts astrology is presented as a universal means of accurately understanding the psychology of an individual human being and of the collective.

It may have seemed that astrology had at last found a respectable niche in modernity as a tool for exploring the human psyche; a tool which utilised rich symbolism, and stimulated the imagination resulting in increased self-awareness and personal growth. The widespread use within psychological astrology of mythology, often Greek, for amplifying astrological placements, connected the individual to their Hellenistic cultural roots, giving an ancient feel to a modern brand of horoscope interpretation.

## AN ASTROLOGY ACCEPTABLE TO MODERNITY?

The view of astrology of James Hillman (1926-2011), founder of the archetypal school of psychology, perhaps comes closest to what could be a respectable and easily justifiable use of astrology in the modern Western world. For Hillman astrology was a rich means of exploring the soul through the captivating symbolism of the astrological chart.[3] Its mythological associations helped the soul re-connect to the broad ideas of psyche standing at the foundation of our culture; it is a means of returning the soul to the gods.

For Hillman, astrology is an art, not an empirical science or objective means of reading psychology. He therefore ruled out any possibility of predicting the future, whether in psychological terms or any other. Whilst emotionally compelling and a powerful means through which the individual can conduct psychological reflection, astrology in Hillman's eyes is a most dangerous thing when taken literally. Its ability to promote sophisticated psychological reflection and develop metaphoric understanding may be countered by the temptation to see it as something necessarily connected to time and the actual movements of the heavens. The base of astrology in astronomical calculations is for Hillman simply a ritual whose purpose is to form a base for the psychological insight then gained. There is no need to explain how astrology works because its purpose is to promote poetic and metaphorical thoughts which help the individual's exploration of their psyche. Astrology thus becomes a method, a tool, making no formal claims about objective reality; it might still be an activity of relatively few persons in modern Western society, but it would at least have a clear and limited rationale.

## THE SCEPTICS DON'T HAVE IT ALL WRONG

Whilst Hillman's view remains one acceptable to modern thought, with astrology an involved, if slightly eccentric way, of imagining one's soul (for which the true modern may prefer the slightly more neutral term, psyche), it is not the view most practising astrologers take. The problem of justifying astrology in modernity remains. Psychological astrologers, as with most of their colleagues in other branches of astrology[4] see the continuous correspondence in time between the heavens and psyche (or possibly just events) as the core doctrine of their subject. In other words, the greater can be read to reveal the lesser, or as classical and Renaissance thinkers expressed it, the macrocosm and the microcosm are related. This holistic nature of the universe, such that one can divine patterns of psyche from patterns of planets, is the philosophical foundation of much of modern Western astrology.

Conceiving the universe holistically, as an interconnected system wherein smaller parts reflect the larger parts, is not however wildly out of line with certain modern theories on the edge of various disciplines. If this rough sort of correspondence were all that astrology contained, it might not be such a controversial subject. One would still have certain problems of course — that meaning and purpose have an objective place in the universe (contrary to the tenets of modern science), and one would have to defend how it was the planets obtained their meanings and whether such meanings can be justified. But there would at least be some sort of core rational base from which to start.

Yet a broad link between planetary pattern and individual life pattern is not all that modern Western astrology contains. It comprises the widespread use of the tropical zodiac, for example, a zodiac that no longer bears a correlation to the constellations in terms of its starting point and which seems to have symbolism suspiciously similar to the pattern of the seasons in the Northern hemisphere. This calls into question its use as a universal, objective system for reading the quality of time in both Northern and Southern hemispheres alike.

It further contains the division of the horoscope into twelve houses or areas of life experience; the method of finding the division being a matter of widespread disagreement between astrologers. Yet further it contains an almost infinite variety of techniques and additional celestial bodies that may be brought in to a chart reading thereby rendering modern (or should we say post-modern) astrological practice an incredibly diverse art.

These controversial and in some cases downright irrational aspects of astrology present thorny problems for those trying to acquaint themselves with the discipline from the vantage point of a modern Western sceptical education. It is no wonder that many open-minded intelligent people shy away from investigating the subject deeply upon encountering such phenomena. That these problematic areas in astrology have not been thoroughly or critically discussed to sufficient degree within astrological communities is hardly a help in astrology's encounter with the modern critical mind.

As I immersed myself in astrology so my journey continued. I enrolled for the MA in Cultural Astronomy and Astrology at the University of Wales and thus began a rich period of critical questioning, of examining the claims astrologers make. I thought long and hard about the philosophy of astrology, and the depth of the underpinning of my own practice. I realised that astrologers are often their own worst enemies, failing to clearly acknowledge the irrational components of their subject. Cast out of the academy for several centuries, there had been little chance for substantial critical evaluation and debate.

## A CASE IN POINT – MERCURY RETROGRADE

Due to the relative rotation of the Earth to the other planets, some planets, from the viewpoint of us here on Earth, periodically appear to travel backwards. When Mercury travels backwards, or as astrologers say, in retrograde motion, it is said to signify mixed communications, periods of review, letters or post going astray, computers playing up, and generally irritating and mischievous happenings around communications, learning and interchange of information. It is common therefore to find astrologers refraining from important communications or decisions during the three annual periods of Mercury's retrograde phase. If any such problems arise during a retrograde phase, the astrologer may be heard commenting with a knowing sigh, 'Ah, Mercury retrograde! What can be done?!'

It takes a minimum of thought to work out that the three periods in the year when Mercury is retrograde cannot be periods of worldwide communications chaos. If they were, bright sparks would have noticed the correlation long ago. It simply is not rational to suggest that on a universal, objective level, the times when Mercury is retrograde are more difficult in Mercury-type activities than any other times for all people in all places.

If this is not a universal phenomenon, then two options present themselves. Firstly, it is not a phenomenon at all and therefore Mercury retrograde periods should be business as usual for astrologers just as for 'normal' people. Secondly, it is a phenomenon that has validity, but not for all people regardless of the condition of their psyche and the quality of the reflecting consciousness they bring to bear on the world. This second option takes us into interesting, possibly taboo, territory. This territory is one that acknowledges astrology's place in the irrational, in the magical world, one that places astrological experience in the subjective realm immune to statistical verification. Yet not subjective in the sense of being unable to give real knowledge or insight. It becomes a mode of engaging with the world that opens a path to mystical experience and dialogue with the cosmos. It becomes something very difficult indeed to define in the usual language of modernity.

## MAKING A LIVING OUTSIDE THE PARADIGM

If the fledgling astrologer wishes to earn a living solely from astrology, then they may be facing a tough challenge. There are no jobs as such in astrology, save for the teaching and managing opportunities provided by the main astrological educational organisations. This means the majority of astrologers will have to cultivate a significant income from marketing themselves as some form of consultant. This raises the further difficulty of trying to create a suitable shell for the sorts of communications that might occur during an astrological reading.

A counsellor who is not quite a counsellor may be the easiest way of being a consulting astrologer in the modern Western world. People understand that there are psychotherapists and counsellors at work in contemporary society. Some astrologers even gain training in these areas and are therefore legitimate in describing themselves as astrological counsellors, although whether the inclusion of astrology in their service is entirely in line with the requirements of their training body is another matter. If the astrologer does not have a formal counselling qualification then they may need to consider a different way of presenting themselves to the paying public.

One different way would be as some form of New-Age therapist and in this guise, the astrologer might sit alongside a Tarot-card reader, a hypnotherapist, a medium, Reiki master or any one of numerous other alternative practitioners in the Mind-Body-Spirit mix of contemporary spiritual culture. The problem here is that the in-depth training of many an astrologer is hardly comparable to that of a Tarot-card reader or three weekends studying Reiki healing. In such a milieu therefore the astrologer may struggle to convey what is often quite a psychologically-sophisticated reading, instead being requested to give short readings that focus on what the future holds for a particular individual.

A third form of astrological consultant might be one who takes the form of a financial or business consultant, who will often give hard practical advice for following say, stock market patterns, in relation to planetary cycles. This is a rare form of consultant, although one which might well be financially successful, mixed as they are with the cash-rich worlds of business, finance and investment.

The truth may be that there is no obvious form of consultation for the budding astrologer to ape and the only choice may be therefore to advertise oneself as an astrologer, alongside detailed information of what that means in this particular case and what will and will not be covered in a reading. The astrologer is in an ill-defined position in modern Western society, located somewhere between counsellor, prophet, priest, and magician. There are few who can truly fulfil this role, and successfully make a living from consultations alone. Yet it is not impossible, and you will read the lives in astrology of two such people in the remaining chapters of this book.

For my own part I was in an unusually fortunate position. Privileged to be at the helm of one of the world's most prestigious astrological schools, and invited to teach on the only MA with astrology in the title in the United Kingdom, I could count myself one of the lucky few who could spend all their working hours on activities related to astrology. Yet a problem remained: the problem of division from that other rather large section of humanity who did not share the worldview in which I operated. What was I to do with this rich, often mystical sense of experience, this knowledge that seemed to have the potential to enlighten and empower, but which so few others could understand? Did I really wish to live entirely in a world which could not be shared by my husband, children and the everyday people I met? I wearied of the difficult and lengthy explanations which followed conversations about what I did, the bafflement of dentist, doctor, council official, mortgage broker and the like as to what one could possibly be doing in relation to astrology in this day and age.

*Prometheus* (Gustave Moreau, 1868)

I faced a paradox. The subject that had opened up a stronger sense of my own soul and its relationship to the cosmos had also alienated me from other human beings and sections of society in which I had previously been comfortable. The archetypes of Uranus, Prometheus and Chiron loomed large. It was time to reassess; Saturn, worldly ruler of my Sun sign Capricorn, was calling.

## URANUS, CHIRON AND PROMETHEUS (AND LET'S NOT FORGET NEPTUNE)

The symbolism associated with Uranus, Chiron and Prometheus stands out as immediately representative of the astrologer in the modern world; the rebel, the wounded one, and the one who is punished for his or her audacity.

First we take Uranus, the planet representing those who are prepared to take intellectual risk, those who think outside the box, who embrace radical ideas, who are unafraid to shock and surprise. Uranus is the pioneer and the cosmic philosopher. Uranus is the very idea of the heavens; 'Ouranos' in Greek literally translates as sky. It is no wonder that Uranus is often identified as the modern ruler of astrology; surely we do indeed need a new ruler of astrology in modernity. It is no longer an accepted mode of interpretation which befits its traditional ruler, Mercury. Instead, it is the voice of the outsider, the radical and the one who is prepared to stand outside the ideas of the status quo.

The minor planet Chiron, discovered in 1977, is known as the wounded healer. Chiron in myth was the wise centaur, who suffered constantly from his wounded thigh but who was ever patient, kind and good. He practised healing, read the stars, and taught others. His wound was one that could never heal, could never be made right; although Chiron was a great healer, he was unable to heal himself. This is a poignant image for the modern astrologer, who is wounded at base level for promoting a cosmology that simply does not align with the prevailing view.

In Prometheus we meet the one who stole the secret of fire from the gods and brought it to humankind. In stealing cosmic knowledge Prometheus incurred the wrath of those gods and determined his fate of eternal punishment. His liver was pecked out daily by an eagle, only for it to regenerate overnight so that each day his torture would start all over again.

The lesson of Prometheus is a chastening one for astrologers. Many astrologers may feel they have knowledge that others require, that can set hearts and minds alight. Yet the crusader who wishes to enlighten others with ideas they would rather forget or ignore may often be ill-received. Further, there may be punishment for daring to look into the secrets of nature and the imagination. The astrologer of any period must be wary of constellating this myth, for to parade one's insight too openly is to incur the wrath of others, perhaps even the wrath of the gods themselves.

And we must not forget Neptune, that slippery, psychic, mysterious and disappearing deity, discovered in planetary form in 1846 at the height of the explosion in spiritualism, mesmerism and ideologies that enchanted generations and changed the world. Neptune symbolises the irrational, mysterious and spiritual sides of astrology, its ability to slip away when analysed too closely, to delude and deceive, and to enchant. In astrology's refusal to be defined by the modern world, and at times to fly in the face of rational common-sense, it is perhaps Neptune who has the last laugh.

## UNEASY INTEGRATION

Eventually, I decided to re-join the world, at least in part. I determined I would combine my astrological interests with those I thought I had left far behind; a mainstream career, the resurrection of old friendships. I scaled down my astrological involvement, not through want of interest but because life's rich tapestry is far wider than those lucky few who have discovered this beautiful art. My astrological chart suggests that other people are vital elements of my own journey. Yet it seemed to me that without a solid footing in the 'real' world, in the mainstream world of modern Western society, I could not meet the variety of people I needed to in order to feel fully connected with the world around me. Having found a connection to the cosmos through astrology, it had started to slip away from me by my losing touch with the wider collective and its concerns.

There are glimmers of hope for contemporary astrology. Recent decades have seen academics posit the breakdown of modernism and entry to a post-modern world in which pluralism and relativism are accepted, in which even such strange practices as contemporary astrology may be seen as just those things that some people do and described in their own terms without unnecessary prejudice. Even Jung, generally dismissed as a mystic and esotericist with little to contribute to academic psychology, is being reappraised in the light of the publication of his *Red Book*; his diary of images and inner experiences detailing his journey to the depths of his own unconscious.

As someone attuned to the symbolic mode of perception through my astrological training, I will always have one foot in and one foot out of the modern world. As Chiron makes five exact passes over my Midheaven, the question of my place in society looms large. I can accept never fully fitting in to any one section of society. Life is imperfect, and we all feel like outsiders on occasion. Whether free or fated, and slightly ill at ease in the modern world or not, I know this: the gift of astrology as a means of connecting with the cosmos is one that remains, however we choose to navigate our way through 21st century life.

### NOTES

1. Thomas Nagel, *The View from Nowhere* (Oxford: Oxford University Press, 1986).

2. Dane Rudhyar, *The Astrology of Personality* (Sante Fe, NM: Aurora Press, 1991 [1936]), p.81.

3. See Hillman's lecture 'Heaven Retains Within Its Sphere Half of All Bodies and Maladies' for full details of his view of astrology.

4. Notable exceptions being Geoffrey Cornelius and Maggie Hyde.

# Chapter Nine
# MY LIFE IN ASTROLOGY
## DARBY COSTELLO

### AMERICA

There is not a place in my memory when I did not know the time of my birth. For some reason, this was information that my mother thought relevant, along with the fact that I was a Gemini. At some point in my childhood Sun-sign columns appeared in the local papers and she read them after breakfast – in the kitchen in the winter, out on the lawn in the summer. This was on the days we didn't walk down the hill to the road where we waited for the bus to school. My youngest siblings don't have this memory, but I was the eldest of five and we lost our parents quite early, so perhaps, had she lived, we would have all grown up with this astrological sense of ourselves.

From mid-teens to my early twenties I was in a Roman Catholic boarding school and later a Catholic college taught by wonderfully intelligent Ursuline nuns and Jesuit priests. I don't remember any astrology there at all, not even in our subversive phases. (We were already reading the then most controversial Pierre Teilhard de Chardin only a few years after his death). But once I was out and free to fly, it seemed to be everywhere. It was the mid-1960s and a new kind of freedom was flourishing amongst the youth of America and Europe. After graduation, I worked in an office for three months to make the money to go to Europe. I planned to travel a bit and then come home to further my education; become Something.

## EUROPE

In October 1967 a college friend and I were standing in Trafalgar Square in our duffle coats and our innocence, open to everything. We had come to 'undo our education' in every way we could. A rather dishevelled young man with a beautiful speaking voice came up and asked for a cigarette and that began an adventure that lasted for years. That summer I ended up on the Isle of Wight working for his splendid Capricorn mother in her hotel and astrology was around to the extent that we all knew each others' signs and she read us our horoscopes every day from the newspaper. One night a cantankerous old man in a pub heard me say something about astrology and began baiting me: 'You just guess what sign I am if you're so smart'. I said, 'I don't need to guess. You're a Taurus'. I was as shocked as everyone else to get it right and responded sweetly and with delight when he bought us a round of cider.

What stands out most powerfully from that time was that there were kindred spirits everywhere. It was mostly the music that bonded us in our youth, and the substances that were floating around that aided us in seeing patterns we might not have noticed without special training!

## AMERICA

By the end of 1968 I was back in America and in early '69 five of us ended up in Yucatan, Central America. We stayed on a remote farm for some months, meditating and eating nothing but fruit and nuts. We lived in an orchard, slept in hammocks, and had ten books between us. It was there that astrology first really found me.

One of the books was about astrology. I've thought for years the book was Jess Stearn's *A Time for Astrology* but the web tells me that was published in 1971, so it cannot have been that book. It was by someone who went to investigate and debunk astrology and ended up falling in love with it. I read it in a hammock amongst the fruit trees. Finishing it, I stood up, walked into the long low hacienda, and said, 'I have to go back to America to find someone who will teach me astrology'. Soon after that, we were forced to leave Mexico in rather dramatic circumstances. We were flown to Dallas, Texas; two of us went to California, and the others returned to the East Coast.

We stayed in San Francisco for about a month and one afternoon a group of us were eating lunch at a long table in a room that had a huge window overlooking the bay. We decided to try to draw an astrological chart. There was an ephemeris and a table of houses left by someone on a shelf and one of us knew something about calculations. Slowly, person after person left the table. In the end, there were just two of us. For some reason he and I would not give up. We stayed there until, at about three in the morning, we got it! We drew up our charts. We'd figured it out. Such a feeling of triumph.

I wanted to stay in San Francisco, but someone said a great astrologer, called Isobel Hickey, was teaching in Boston. So when a car was going back to Massachusetts, I got in. Once back, I got distracted and went to New Hampshire to hang out with the Baba Ram Dass crowd. There I met a young man who did my chart. He said I should study astrology, that I was made for it and he would teach me. 'Great chat-up line', I thought.

The only other thing I remember is sitting in a field one day, weeping for a long time. I had been given Dane Rudhyar's *The Pulse of Life* and read it in a day and then had a powerful dream that night which I now can't remember. But there in the field with *The Pulse of Life* in my hands I knew I wasn't going to go on to get an MA and then a PhD; I wasn't going to return to a 'normal' life, all mapped out by my background. For some reason I felt this as a loss, very powerfully, on that day; I wept for the loss of a 'predictable' future and at the beauty of that book.

And so I went to Boston and found Isobel Hickey in June of 1969. Her reading cost $10. She said I was an astrologer born and must come and study with her. I remember thinking, 'Do they all say this?' But I listened with fascination. She told me her next class began in September and I should go and study with Francis Sakoian and Louis Acker for the summer, then come to her in September. Years later, I found out that they were not friends and it was unheard of that she would send me to them. I think she was afraid I would get distracted (being a Gemini!) and go off elsewhere, but she was sure I should come to her to study and become an astrologer.

When a new friend asked me what I needed in order to stay and study, I told her: a flat, preferably with an astrology student, a job and a bicycle. She found all three for me within a month. My flatmate was a delightful person (Capricorn again) who was also studying with Isobel; amazing grace!

My job was as a secretary at the Massachusetts Institute of Technology (M.I.T.). My bicycle was blue.

I began studying with Frances and Louis immediately. They were so exciting! And when Isobel started her classes in September, I carried on with them and also studied with her. My strongest memory of her teaching is the 'prayer' we said before starting – it invoked protective deities for our work, and made us aware that this was a sacred task. She taught re-incarnational astrology and she told us that we had been in Atlantis and had not paid attention and Atlantis had collapsed. We were incarnated here again at another critical time and we must not fail in guiding people to pay attention, because if it collapsed this time, it might not recover. She made us feel the responsibility very keenly.

Today I would not use the language that was natural to us then in describing our work or ourselves. But the sense of our responsibility has never left me nor the people I still know who studied with her in those years: the awareness of the sacred art we were learning, its antiquity, and the necessity of using it well. I am eternally grateful to her for instilling that responsibility in us.

All of the people I associated with during those years were familiar with astrology – or if they were not, I never knew it, nor would it have occurred to me to have a friend that was anti-astrology. Nathalie, whose flat I shared, and I were a centre of social activity. In fact, that is where I first met Howard Sasportas. He was a regular and most engaging visitor! (When I left Boston, and America, he told me he was now going to study astrology too – he would go to England and study with the Faculty of Astrological Studies). The food was always good (Nathalie was a brilliant vegetarian cook) and the conversations exhilarating. Of course, I knew there were people 'out there' who thought our 'esoteric' way of seeing reality was foolish. After all, I was working at M.I.T. while studying in the evenings. I was one of three secretaries in the psychiatry department – there were thirteen psychiatrists for the brilliant and highly-strung students, in those days.

All of the psychiatrists knew I was studying astrology, but I never experienced aggression about it from any of them, although there was one who was sceptical – he questioned me endlessly. He was a Gemini, like me, and we sparred energetically. The others seemed to find it more or less interesting. A few wholly supported my studies, and I remember them with great affection. They found it much more disturbing that I would not join the anti-war marches – that I was not 'political'. My 19-year-old brother was in Vietnam and I was writing to him constantly and I knew that he would be hurt if I was part of that movement. The politics of the time were so powerful, as was the feminist movement, and I was verbally attacked by passionate adherents of both for not joining them. It was an intense time for all of us.

My office, 1972-78

## SOUTH AFRICA

In January of 1971, having learned as much as I could from my wonderful teachers, I left Boston, and America. Several months later, I found myself in Johannesburg, South Africa. It was time for a change and someone I'd met in Europe invited me to come down there, so I thought I'd go for a visit. Isobel warned me that if I left then, June of 1971, I would not get back to

America for a very long time, as my progressed Sun was on my Saturn. I stayed in South Africa for twelve years.

It was in Johannesburg where I really began to practise the art of astrology. Within about three months of arriving, people began asking me to read their charts. I never said no. And never charged anyone money. After about eighteen months, I was doing several charts a week, always after coming home from the museum where I was recording and transcribing the lore and practices of the sangomas.[1]

One day, on a visit to Cape Town, I met a woman named Delphica, who, I think, was in her seventies. She'd lived in London in her youth, and studied astrology with the Theosophists. After spending a weekend with her, she said, 'You must begin charging money'. She had never done that, for philosophical reasons, plus a lack of confidence, and, anyway, she had inherited enough money to live modestly.

She told me if I dared to charge people for doing their charts, 'In five years you will learn more than I have learned in fifty'. Such a dramatic statement! I returned to Jo'burg in mid-December and in January of 1973 an artist named Clarence Wilson[2] came to me and at the end of the session he said, 'How much do you charge?'; I said, 'I don't'. And he took out a ten rand note and handed it to me, saying 'You do from now'. And from then, I did.

When I began doing charts the client and I sat on cushions on the floor with notes I'd taken in preparation, and some books I'd brought from America all around us. I used the notes and books as I went along. Right from the beginning I used a 'format' that I still use (though I no longer sit on the floor nor do I quote from books much): I would give the person paper to take notes and then just start talking about the chart, saying everything I could about the chart in front of me. After some minutes, when I could think of nothing more to say, I would look up and ask the person if it made sense so far, or I would simply ask a question about something I had seen. Looking back, I can see that there were two reasons that led me to this approach. Every day I was with the sangomas who were telling me about their practices. At some point, once I had become trusted as a person who was truly 'working with the spirits' (the extraordinary Credo Mutwa formally named me Nonokanyazi, 'Child of the Stars'), a beloved sangoma named Dorcas asked me why white doctors asked so many questions when you went to them. 'Da, shouldn't they know what is wrong with you?' She asked this because the sangomas were taught to 'see' what the person had come for — sometimes they used the bones[3] and sometimes the insights which they accessed through trance. A big part of their training was the development of what we would call intuition; day after day, the twasas (initiates) were trained to find things that had been hidden. Seeing them work that way, I fell into the same habit. I had the chart in front of me. I had the person in front of me. Why should I not see what they needed me to see? As I did it for free for the first eighteen months, I used that time to refine my ability to gather the various pieces of 'information' in the chart into my heart's mind — planets, aspects, etc. — and then let it flow out to the other person. Because I was not charging money, I could say, 'It's important you tell me when I get it wrong, because you are part of my learning now'. Over time, my ability to leap from bits of information to a clear image became refined and after a time I began recording the sessions for people.

During this period I became close to a woman who was fascinated by Carl Jung and even more, James Hillman. (She later went to the Jung Institute in Zurich, and became an analyst). I began reading deeply. I'd read Jung at university, having majored in psychology (with philosophy and theology as minors), but this was different. Yvonne was steeped in Jung and we talked for hours, every moment I was not in the museum or with the sangomas or doing charts. And somehow, the combination of these conversations — with the sangomas and with Yvonne drew me away from the reincarnational view of the chart towards something more ancestral and archetypal. I was beginning to see ancestral influences in the chart and how they were brought to life through the psychological interactions of the parents with each other and the child when the person whose chart I was doing was very young. With every chart I learned something new.

Soon I was doing charts of the spouses, children, parents, lovers, friends of everybody I'd seen — Johannesburg's English-speaking community was a relatively small one and it seemed to me everyone knew everyone else. And that led me to the one rule that has so far been unbreakable[4]: the rule of confidentiality. From quite early on I realised that not only must I keep people's secrets, I must keep their identities secret. It was also because I realised that if I consulted someone and I thought they might tell their spouse or friends about me, I'd not like it. So that meant I could not tell anyone at all. And so the habit developed. I know that now many astrologers have supervisors and I suppose the closest I got to this was a combination of Yvonne and the sangomas. But still I never revealed names – not even to Yvonne, even though she was a rare outsider not integrated into the community; she was a loner. I talked to the sangomas about awkward clients, without naming them, and that was immensely helpful too. The sangomas taught me so much about dealing with people who came to me for guidance.

The big test of my confidentiality principle was doing the chart of a very famous person, a great film star and not being able to tell anyone afterwards. I remember that I shook with the tension of it when I saw my friend, Yvonne, but I got through it and the habit became easier with time. In general, I learned to wait for a few days and then tell her I'd seen someone with this or that difficulty and I'd dealt with it this or that way. Then we'd discuss it, her from the psychological point of view and me from the astrological. Also when I had really difficult people I would ask one of the sangomas how they would deal with such a person. I learned so much from them, about how to deal with what we call 'boundary issues' today.

The conversations with Yvonne also made me aware that to do this work I must be prepared to face myself, my own hidden sides. When a client was too much like me, I'd either love them or judge them without understanding that. When they were too unlike me, I'd try to find where they were like me so I could identify with them. I became aware that if I had trouble with a client, it may not be the client, it may be something in myself that could not see the client with clarity and compassion. If I liked someone too much, it may be that my vanity was being activated. Self-reflection became a daily task which is now a lifetime habit. Sad to admit, I still fall into the same traps – but the recognition is often so quick now that I'm able to fling myself back to the middle space of compassionate objectivity – at least I hope that is true. There have been three incidences in my life as an astrologer where I have told the person to leave, not allowing them to pay me, so unable was I to find compassion for their actions. They were shocked, and so was I, but I knew I had to do that at the time.

At some point during this period, Liz Greene's book *Saturn* arrived in my hands. I read every word with my heart singing and felt that for the very first time I had 'met' someone who was seeing astrology – describing the work of it – in a way that lit up my mind and touched my soul. It was so exciting. I read it out loud to everyone I saw for a long time.

After I'd been doing people's charts for some time, 'forecasting' had become a real problem. People kept wanting me to see into their futures. I only wanted to see how I might help them with their difficulties, inner or outer. (I had not developed the notion of 'navigating by the stars' yet). I kept saying, 'I don't do forecasting', and they would say, 'but you can see where the planets will be in a year – what do they say?' I had the feeling that it would be somehow wrong to look at the future that way and, worse, what if I could actually see the future? I didn't want that gift. And what about Free Will? My Catholic background was rising to the surface![5]

At that time I was not yet reading 'deep texts' but just whatever took my fancy. I came across a book by Frank Herbert called *Dune*. And then I read the sequel, *Dune Messiah*. By the end of the book I felt I could look at the future. I don't remember the details but I remember thinking this: There is an almost inevitable destiny that is inborn in each of us. But, if we are able and willing to look at ourselves and willing and able to exercise immense discipline we might veer away from the ingrained direction and choose another version, or even an unknown version. There might be moments when such a decision is possible, and even feels necessary. Most people would simply live out their given natures. However, some might feel the necessity of breaking away, for the good of themselves or of others.

This is simplifying the vision I took from the book, but it illuminated my imagination. I began to see that ongoing transits and progressions could be a way of working with one's fate, or destiny, rather than just living it out. We could use the chart for soul work – get to know our natures so that we might bring out the finest possibilities through working with progressions and transits throughout our lives. One day I heard myself say to a person with a non-Saturnian chart who was experiencing a heavy Saturn aspect, 'You can feel cramped and stuck or you can dedicate this time to a particular practice, a discipline, so that when Saturn moves on you will have more ability to carry things through. And you will find yourself to be more rigorous in the pursuits of your aim. Find someone to complain to and then just do the work!' And I taught myself to follow my own advice – to experiment constantly with how things might work. (Now I would say, 'to cultivate the nature one was given'). When Rob Hand's book on Transits came into my hands, I leapt with excitement again – I read the relevant bits of it to every client that came to me.

There was a time in Johannesburg when it seemed that people wanted me to be a guru. At that point I was not even teaching yet, just doing charts, day after day. I noticed this the first time when, at a party, a woman I'd seen as a client criticised me when I told her I'd felt horrible all week, but was suddenly feeling better having fun at the party. How could I feel horrible when I knew so much? Over the years this sort of thing has happened again and again in various ways. Sometimes people have 'fallen in love' with the wonderful astrologer, and then invited her home and over time become disillusioned with the ordinary creature I can be, when I am not being wise and splendid! It never stops upsetting me, but I learned long ago that I must not defend myself against people because they might do that. When someone whom I've taught or whose chart I've done gets to know me in another context I take the chance that it might or might not work. Some of my dearest friends first saw me as astrologer, teacher, wise person. Over the years they have gotten to know my fragile and annoying sides, and when they can accept this, our friendships have deepened. But sometimes that doesn't happen, and I am a great disappointment. I'll continue to risk that because of the generally wonderful things that happen. And of course, over time, I have discovered that I can do the same thing to others – after finding someone magical, I have lost interest and slipped away. We always do what we see done to us, in one way or another, it seems to me.

When I'd been in Jo'burg about eight years, a woman who had invited me to give some classes in her home got frustrated with me one evening and said, 'Why won't you let us make you a guru? It's so annoying!' It's really because I'm not the type – can't follow one, can't be one. I see myself as a mixed creature, alternating between being psychologically frail and strong, with a wonderful gift that I do my best to honour in every way I can. And I won't let anyone get close to me who does not honour my gift, as I hope always to honour their particular gift.

In 1978 the man with whom I shared everything, including my life with the sangomas, died. I retreated from that world, and mourned deeply. Some time later, the sangoma to whom I was closest also died. Her name was Ndlaleni Cindi. In my heart, I left Africa then. But it took some time for life to bring the next opportunity. My astrology work kept me alive – I had so very many interesting people coming to me. And a few friends with whom I shared companionship and love.

## LONDON

In 1983, one of these beloved friends (who later became my husband) and I came to London. He wanted a change, and I was aching for conversations with astrologers. I was sure I'd find them in London after a dream about a London bookshop where people met in the back to talk astrology. On waking I longed to find that bookshop, knowing there must be a community of astrologers there. I only knew three people in London; Howard (Sasportas), Liz (Greene) (whom I'd met on my one trip to London) and a friend called Bridget.[6]

Through work, grace, and Bridget's clear guidance, we found and moved into part of a house in Hampstead owned by a German artist who had fled Nazi Germany with her husband and companions in the 1940s. Crystal was in her mid-70s and not only fascinating, but magical. She loved astrology and she sent all of her friends to me. One day we were talking about our mothers and I described her mother through her Moon and Venus positions and aspects. The next day we met by chance on the street. In passing she said, 'Thank you for helping me with my mother' (who had died decades ago). I said, 'Still??' She grinned and said, 'Forever'. I learned so much from her and her friends who were in their 70s, 80s and 90s.

Living in London fulfilled everything I dreamed of, although I never stopped missing South Africa and its indigenous people. Finding the astrological community here, with its multi-varied ways of doing astrology, its clan allegiances, its endless rifts and reconciliations, its gatherings and opportunities felt like a blessing beyond reckoning. I had the idea that if I learned to lecture and to write then I would have access to the best astrological conversations in the world. Slowly over the years I learned to teach, lecture and give seminars – starting at home with small groups, endlessly asking for criticism from those I trusted. Invited by Liz and Howard to teach at the CPA in 1987 gave me a perfect home within the community. With Liz's encouragement I began writing books for the CPA Press. In 1988 I was invited to teach in Cologne, and from then, teaching

The young astrologer and the young sangoma: Ndlaleni Cindi and me, c. 1973.

in other countries became part of my life as an astrologer. Like many others, I have travelled the world teaching – and learning – each country having its own cultural colours that we have to recognise and honour when interpreting the patterns in the heavens for their people.

Another richness of that period was becoming part of a small group at the Company of Astrologers, led by Graham Tobyn, translating medieval Latin astrological texts into English. It lasted for seven years and began a life-time love affair with ancient texts, going back farther and farther into antiquity where some of the roots of our art had their first appearances.

In 1989, Jim Lewis, of Astro*Carto*Graphy fame, came to London and gave a brilliant talk on the Saturn-Uranus-Neptune in Capricorn conjunction in terms of its historical implications. He ignited a passion for collective historical cycles in my heart and mind and opened my awareness to the outer planets in a wholly new way. It changed my teaching and the way I did charts from then on, allowing me to weave the individual and personal life into the larger cycle and into a new tapestry of understanding.

In the early 1990s I began teaching at the Faculty and, through the years, have found this to be another beloved home for my heart and mind.

In the 2000s I began working with Frank Clifford and The London School of Astrology with its again very different and delightful teachers and students. And it was also in the first decade of the new millennium that the MA in Cultural Astronomy and Astrology was born at Bath Spa

University. Many of us became part of it with such excitement – some of us teaching it, and others of us becoming students of the cultural history of our ancient stellar art.[7]

It seems that the astrological world has deepened and expanded beyond anything I could have imagined in the 1960s. However, it was not really until London that I realised what being such an 'outsider' meant in my life. In South Africa, working with the sangomas and being an astrologer were just who I was. I met lots of people with conventional attitudes there, but somehow being different was just not a problem. A year after arriving in England I was invited to a somewhat 'grand' dinner party in Kensington. I was used to my wonderful landlady and her interesting artistic friends, but had not met very many conventional English people yet. My host introduced me as 'a rather wonderful astrologer' and the woman who took my hand looked at me down her long nose and said, in the most Maggie Smith Downton Abbey'ish way, 'Aoooo, how quaint!' I later told my friend, our host, never to introduce me as an astrologer again, unless I decided it was OK! And I never again told anyone I was an astrologer unless I thought the conversation would be interesting. It's easier than one thinks: most people are distracted when you are truly interested in their lives and opinions. Having said this, I've had some of the most interesting and unexpected conversations with people at dinner tables all over England once I decided to tell them I was an astrologer.

Of course it is often known that I am an astrologer when I come into a group of people. Again, early on, I was very clear that I would never allow astrology or myself as an astrologer to be disrespected. As soon as it's mentioned, I become very alert and attentive. Once, at a party, I was introduced to the Astronomer Royal, and people stood around, rather looking forward to a sharp encounter as someone asked him his opinion about astrology. I went into my alert, slow-motion attention. But I needn't have worried. He was incredibly graceful at diffusing the tension – and I followed his gentle lead – and as the group dispersed we had a brief but delightful conversation together about the intermixed history of our beloved but now divorced, disciplines. I have found that really intelligent people are rarely frightened of astrology.

Over the years, I have become aware of the growing desire of many people in the astrological community to be accepted into the conventional world. Having consciously left the conventional world, yet being of service within it, albeit often secretly, this seems to me a great freedom. It once upset me when a regular client, the head of an organisation, said, 'I could never put you on my published board of advisors'. In time I have become grateful for that. It seems right to live outside the tribes – in the vast spaces of the stars, observing the ever-changing patterns in their mystery and wonderment. It seems right to then come deep into the heart of the world, with all the various types of people who find us and can use our help at navigating by the stars – and then to return to contemplation and wonder. It feels right not to be constrained by the demands of a conventional professional life and the limits it would impose on us if we joined them.

I see the astrological world expanding, adapting and deepening, I am glad to have been part of its return into culture, but also glad to be an 'elder' now – listening, attending, witnessing the new generations of astrologers as they rise up, bringing new insights and inspirations to our sacred art. I find myself to be a fierce critic, for better or worse, of any astrology that is not aimed towards guidance in what I call 'the work of love'. But I am also willing to listen, to learn from anyone who is dedicated to our ancient and sacred art and called to its depth and beauty. That matters more than anything else – and those who are its servants are my family.

### NOTES

1. This is another story, and some of it is told to Gary Phillipson in an interview for *The Mountain Astrologer* in 2004 which is on my website darbycostello.co.uk and on skyscript.co.uk. More of this story is described in an essay called, 'The Call of the Spirit: The Training and Practice of Sangomas in Relation to an Astrologer's Vocation' in *Daimonic Imagination: Uncanny Intelligence*, ed. by Angela Voss and William Rowlandson. (Cambridge: Cambridge Scholars Publishing, 2013).

2. Clarence is an exception to my rule of silence as he and I dined out on this encounter many times in the following years in the various social circles we shared. He died in the 1980s. He was a wonderful artist and delightful person and I shall always remember him for his Cancerian concern and his Leo rising way of giving me courage.

3. The 'bones' are the divination tools of many sangomas. They are bits of bone, stones, ivory, shells, gathered over time and they are thrown on the ground and the patterns they make give information to the sangoma about the person asking guidance. I once asked Dorcas what it was that I was doing, and she said, 'Da, in the beginning God threw the bones (she gestured to the stars) and you read them'.

4. With one or two exceptions where I have had permission.

5. At university we read Thomas Aquinas, of course, but I don't think we read his words on astrology. Years later, in London, I went to see a priest to ask him if being an astrologer kept me out of the Church. (I wasn't sure that I wanted to be 'in the Church' but I wanted to know my position, if I ever chose to participate in its rituals again). He asked me many questions about how I dealt with 'seeing the future in the stars' and I told him how I tried to help people to get to know their natures so they might exercise their 'free will' in situations where instincts and desires might lead them to actions they would regret in their pursuit of excellence. At the time I was becoming fascinated by the ancient Greek notion of arete in its association with the inherited or learned ability to choose honourable behaviour over brutish behaviour. This word *arete* (Greek ἀρετή) seemed to denote the essence of things and the assumption was that the true essence of a human was to choose what I thought of at that time as Excellence. He told me that I was doing nothing against the teachings of the Church and in fact, helping people to see their natures and their choices was very good work. He must have read Aquinas and the passage which describes how the wise man rules his stars as opposed to the unwise man who does not chose to go against his instincts and desires. (*Summa Theologica, I,I 115 4 AD Tertium (5.544)*). In spite of beginning to understand something about fate, destiny and free will, I still find it something of a mystery. In 2005 when I was studying for my MA in Cultural Astronomy and Astrology at Bath Spa University, I wrote a paper on '*Fate and Free Will*' so I could think about it all over again. I enjoyed the research immensely. These days I still love the big questions, but no longer require answers.

6. She had come to South Africa from London with Tony Buzan (of Mind Mapping fame) and Michael Gelb to help with a project I'd become deeply involved with to do with education for children in Soweto.

7. This later became the MA in Cultural Astronomy and Astrology at the University of Wales, Trinity Saint David. See uwtsd.ac.uk/sophia

Chapter Ten
# A LIFE ASTROLOGICAL
## MELANIE REINHART

Anyone who listens to BBC Radio 4 will recognise this title as a wordplay on one of its regular features, 'A Life Scientific'. Shamelessly copying this programme, where scientists offer personal anecdotes, in this essay I do likewise, also reflecting on things metaphysical, and musing upon questions largely unanswerable. However, quite unlike 'A Life Scientific', all this is underpinned with astrological references!

### THE JOURNEY BEGINS

My astrological journey began in 1959 at the age of ten, in the Bulawayo Public Library – a motley collection, mostly about the hazards of farming in sub-Saharan Africa, the usual classics of English Literature, some obscure Africana of dubious scholarship, and so on. However, one shelf called out to my interest in metaphysics, already stimulated by encountering the Christian dogma as taught at the convent school I attended. I simply refused to accept the notion that those who did not go 'by the way of Jesus' (here meaning literally becoming confirmed Christians) would suffer damnation. And none of the grown-ups seemed able to provide satisfactory answers to my anguished questions. Perhaps it will not surprise the reader to learn that this occurred at my first Chiron-Chiron square, with natal Chiron in Sagittarius.

But here, in the library, the contents of this single shelf entitled 'Philosophy, Psychology and Religion' offered a door to another world, full of inspiring ideas about life and the human soul. I noticed a small book on astrology, pulled it off the shelf and began reading. I soon felt a wave of indignation. Somehow, I absolutely knew there was more to astrology than was described in these pages, and I set about finding out for myself. One of my great regrets is that I do not recall the title of this little book. What fun it would be now to see what provoked such outrage in my ten-year-old mind!

## THE NEXT STEP

Having memorised the signs of the zodiac and their associations, I asked everyone I met about their birth date. I tried to see how their behaviour and personality related to the brief descriptions I had read. Lacking at first any other reading material, astrology classes or intellectual milieu, I just noticed … and noticed … and noticed … and meanwhile, went on a journey of learning about what people of other faiths believed. My first port of call was the Spiritualist Church, where I was taken under the wing of Frieda Kroeger, a gifted full-trance medium, clairvoyant and healer. She was my first mentor, and this early exposure to things 'other-dimensional' has continued to inform my astrology practice to this day.

## UNDER THE RADAR

In 1968, I went to the University of Cape Town to study for a degree in the Humanities. The stunning location and wondrously expanded social environment contrasted starkly with the ugliness and violence of apartheid, then in its heyday. Censorship was in force, and a great many books were banned, for reasons moral, political or philosophical. However, the local bookshop used to alert us via the 'bush telegraph' when shipments were due of titles they knew would soon be axed by the censors. And we students would flock in and buy them before they disappeared. We developed a 'citizens' library', circulating books by Timothy Leary, Jack Kerouac, Alan Watts, Allen Ginsberg, Ram Dass, Franz Fanon, R.D. Laing, D.H. Lawrence and many others whose writings were shaping the then-contemporary world of 'Flower Power'. We rocked to Jimi Hendrix, Janis Joplin, the Rolling Stones and The Who, among many of the 'greats' of the 1960s. We aspired to 'Make Love Not War', as a tiny minority who were neither pro-apartheid, nor committed to the anti-apartheid path of political activism.

We learned to stay 'under the radar' in order to avoid the machinations of the notorious 'Special Branch', the secret police who targeted the student population, hunting out those with views not congruent with the prevailing political system — and sometimes destroying their lives. Many years later, as a fledgling professional astrologer, I read of souls far braver and greater than myself who suffered imprisonment or who eloquently defended our profession (and their own reputation) in court.[1] And I vowed to never knowingly allow myself to be put in a position where I was required to prove anything to anyone. Not ever.

In the late 1960s, Uranus was just separating from its conjunction with Pluto in Virgo, and 'the revolution' was starting. Our slogan was 'The only way out is UP!', encapsulating our belief that the power of spiritual awakening was the only 'remedy' for the travails of a violent society which in turn had been extruded from oppressive and adversarial philosophical beliefs. This highly charged milieu offered a fertile field in which the seeds of astrology, already planted in my life some ten years earlier, could grow. Writing now, I can see how this prepared me for a life of being willing to stay 'under the radar' in service to the profession of astrology. Colonial Rhodesia eventually transformed in 1980 into independent Zimbabwe, but that is another story. Suffice it to say that the serial tragedies which have befallen my beautiful homeland have taught me about the fragility of all cultural and historical forms. The enduring nature of the 'Perennial Wisdom', as Aldous Huxley called it, became a necessary reality for me.[2]

## EPIPHANY

While still in Cape Town, I was given a copy of Dane Rudhyar's book *The Pulse of Life*, and what I read about my Sun sign changed the course of my life. Suddenly, my personal struggles had meaning, set in the context of the 'great round' of the whole zodiac, which in turn was the filter for the incoming cosmic energies of life itself. I was not alone, but a participant in the Great Mysteries.

This sense has never left me, to this day. I wept with joy and relief, and read the book from cover to cover, my mind scintillating at the exquisite prose and the profound ideas so elegantly expressed with such verity and immediacy. With gratitude and a full heart, I committed myself in that moment to following wherever this golden thread would lead.

*Finding the point where heaven and earth touch* (Flammarion, 1888)

## SERENDIPITY

In my graduation year, it became increasingly clear to me that my place was neither in South Africa, nor in Rhodesia. UDI had been declared in 1965,[3] and my parents, with a prophetic eye, encouraged both me and my sister to get a foothold somewhere 'out of Africa'. I decided to go to England. Before leaving, I was introduced to the teachings of the Sufi mystic Hazrat Inayat Khan, in the form of an invitation to contact Murshid Fazal Inayat Khan, then the lineage holder and focal teacher of a community living in Surrey.[4] I wondered what it would be like to meet a spiritual teacher. I was already familiar with the notion that 'When the disciple is ready, the teacher appears'. Was I ready? And how I would know?

Once in England, I attended a lecture given by Fazal. The venue was Friend's House, Euston, London, and the year was 1971. Little did I know then that at the Saturn Return of this event, I would be teaching astrology in this very room! When Fazal appeared and spoke on the theme of 'Within, Without, Throughout' I was transfixed. It seemed that he was speaking to me and me alone, although from the audience responses it was clear that many people felt the same way. During a personal interview with him, I was granted permission to spend a period of time in his community.

## APPRENTICESHIP

During my first week there, I was astounded to discover that Fazal was the director of Servire Publications, then the major publisher of Dane Rudhyar's work! The community library contained a collection of his seminal titles such as *The Astrology of Personality*, *The Astrological Study of Psychological Complexes*, *New Mansions for New Men* and *Triptych*. As nobody else in the community was specifically interested in astrology, I pursued my studies mostly in solitude. I felt as if I had died and gone to heaven!

However, community life was often very far from 'heaven', seeming at times more like 'purgatory'. But it offered an exquisite laboratory situation within which to observe human life 'in the raw'. Once I was able to draw up charts, I had access to many people eager to discuss their horoscopes. I saw how the peaks and troughs of community life perfectly illustrated the various transits of the planets. And specific individual events could be understood as reflections of these cosmic patterns, as people went through the intense personal changes brought about by living in close proximity to each other, and also, crucially, to a very high voltage teacher. I am eternally grateful for this intense, albeit solitary, apprenticeship. It deeply influenced the way I understand astrology, the way I have worked with clients, and the way I have taught students.

Although my mind flew high with Rudhyar's exquisite vision, this astrological apprenticeship was of an eminently practical nature, grounded in observation and application. I learned calculation by studying *Waite's Astrological Compendium*, but the rest of my early astrological 'diet' consisted entirely of the work of Dane Rudhyar.[5] And from Fazal, I learned about knowledge 'inside out' – experience sensed and inwardly felt, only later clothed in words. A very 'lunar' way of learning, befitting Fazal's Sun, Jupiter and Mercury in the sign of Cancer, sitting appropriately in the 9th house of my own horoscope, with his Sun conjunct my MC! I did not know then that twenty years later I would be co-leading experiential workshops with Darby Costello in this very location.[6]

## SATURN CALLS

In the intense, but somewhat isolated environment of community life in the countryside, I had no knowledge of the astrology network in England, its deep roots and wonderful learning opportunities. But one day, a friend gave me a copy of Liz Greene's masterpiece on Saturn.[7] Another epiphany! I marvelled at the beauty of her blend of psychological and esoteric wisdom. Being aware that my Saturn Return was approaching, and understanding something of what this meant, I felt the need to consolidate and deepen my studies. Saturn had called, and I responded by signing up for the Certificate course of the Faculty of Astrological Studies. By this time, I had read many horoscopes, and had been immersed in astrology for about seventeen years, so it was relatively easy to fit into the structure of the course.

## URANUS OVER THE ASCENDANT

The transit of Uranus over my Ascendant meant goodbye to community life, and a move to the big city of London. By then, I was working on the Faculty Diploma course. I joined the Astrological Association and attended their conference in 1977, the very autumn that Chiron was discovered, and began to participate in astrological events. Most inspiring were the workshops run by Liz Greene, then with the Centre for Transpersonal Astrology, in association with the late Ian Gordon-Brown and Barbara Somers. On the first one I attended, I met Barbara Sherrington, a fellow Gemini also doing the Diploma, and we became study partners. A most enjoyable way to discover that if you want to learn something, offer to teach it! We each took the parts of the course we were stuck with, learned them, then taught them to each other during long days of conversation, shared meals and getting to know each other. We are still friends to this day.

## BECOMING PROFESSIONAL

Looking back, I do not recall a 'moment' when I decided to become 'a professional'. It was rather a logical outcome of following the thread I had caught hold of back in the library, all those years ago. Indeed, I believe that astrology is not really a 'career choice' – rather, it is a vocation, a 'calling'. Progressed Venus was separating from my natal Uranus by only a few arc minutes when I fell in love with astrology. Uranus had called! Passion is needed to endure the high level of challenge brought about by the discipline and rigour necessary to follow this path. If one is called to offer service as a consulting astrologer, in addition to the joy of learning and being involved with celestial energies, administrative efficiency and dedication to painstaking astrological work is needed. But, crucially, doing this work also requires an on-going process of self-enquiry whether alone, with colleagues or a supervisor – preferably all three! It is a much accelerated path of awakening if one takes it seriously and supports it with spiritual practices.[8]

## LONDON IN THE 1980s

Liz Greene and Howard Sasportas were giving seminars. Wonderful, thrilling, interesting, inspiring Sundays spent immersed in astrology, with fellow lovers of our great art. The needs of my own process, plus the requirement of my psychotherapy training, meant entering an extended period of therapy of various kinds, both individually and in groups. This included Psychosynthesis, Gestalt Therapy, Transactional Analysis, Jungian Analysis and Primal Integration Therapy. I loved some of it and hated some of it. But the years of exposure to the often messy and painful substrata of my own psyche taught me more about the application of astrology to the inner journey of the soul than any book I had read. Astrology was my guiding light during this period. With one or two notable exceptions, I was not able to share this with my therapists, which although disappointing at the time, now seems totally appropriate.

In learning astrology, a deep, powerful and personal feeling of 'being taught' occurs when connections are spontaneously seen between the microcosm of human experience and the cosmic macrocosm. And for this, a conscious grounding in the deeper realms of our own experience is necessary. Indeed, in these 'aha' moments, it is as if 'Astrology Itself' speaks and the Hermetic maxim, of 'as above, so below' is fulfilled. But in order to hear astrology speaking, we need to learn to be silent within ourselves. And a lot of 'inner noise' may be encountered as we reach towards that silence. But dealing with that is the Work …

*Hermetic Silence* (Achille Bocchi, 1574)

This famous etching depicts Harpocrates, the god of silence, blended with Hermes wearing his winged helmet, holding an index finger to his lips, in a gesture indicating silence.[9] This is sometimes interpreted as secrecy, implying secret societies or occult brotherhoods. However, from Shimon Ben Halevi, a scholar of the Kabbalah, I learned a wonderful definition of the word 'occult'. Usually given the meaning of 'hidden', Halevi offers the following delightful elaboration: 'The word 'occult' refers to 'Something hidden by virtue of the fact that it is so obvious that everyone misses it'.[10]

This notion became something of a guiding principle for me in the art of astrological interpretation. Focus on the obvious, the proverbial 'elephant in the room', allows what is hidden to reveal itself in an organic way. Often astounding or amusing, it always has a ring of truth and relevance. 'You couldn't make this stuff up!' is a quip often spoken by astrologers amazed by the luminous and uncontrived demonstrations of meaning and connectedness which frequently appear in the workings of astrology.

## CHIRON

I heard about the discovery of Chiron in early 1978, when the first ephemeris appeared. I was intrigued, as I knew from Greek mythology about the wise centaur who mentored the Greek heroes, and who was famous for his initially unhealing wound. The shaman. I recalled my teenage years, coping with a serious disease for which I eventually refused treatment after reading about the side-effects of the drugs prescribed. I knew there had to be another way. Within a few months I was symptom-free, thanks to the skill of the only 'alternative health' clinic in Southern Rhodesia at that time. Crucially, I learned how mind and emotion interact with the physical body, and my previous metaphysical reading became grounded in the urgency to become well again. My life was shaped by this illness and, through the healing, I had stepped forever out of the 'mainstream world'.

Checking the ephemeris, I noticed that Chiron was approaching a long series of conjunctions to all my personal planets, through Taurus and Gemini. Little did I know that another illness awaited me! Meanwhile, I began including Chiron in charts, although not interpreting it as I had no idea what to say. But I observed, collected notes, meditated, thought, and wondered.

Then in 1984, the very week that Chiron first entered Gemini, I was taken ill with pneumonia. Gemini is associated with the lungs; transiting Chiron was approaching my Sun, in opposition to its natal place. It had recently squared natal Saturn, the 'Grim Reaper', and my father had died the year before. Here indeed was the wound of the loss of the father. In a delirium, I received a vision and was given an invisible thread to find my way to healing. Following this took me through the 'nether regions' of what Jung termed the 'collective unconscious', revealing both the historical miasma that emerge during cultural shifts, and also the archetypal images they enshroud and eventually awaken. Here was Chiron. Suffering and healing, both personal and collective.

After this, many clients came with 'Chiron stories' to tell. Most had never heard of Chiron, but they offered the most precise and touching demonstrations of its process, via transits to the horoscope, and in their life stories. The mythology and meaning took shape before my eyes and the literalness was often breath-taking. It was the openness and sincerity of these people that taught me about the outworking of Chiron's process. You can doubt, twist, or even fabricate interpretations. However, you cannot fake the manifest and precise symbolism of live occurrences that can be seen to coincide with transits. Although I collected an endless amount of material, the suggestion to write a book came much later, from Howard Sasportas, a dear friend and mentor who I had met in 1980 during my Psychosynthesis training. I set about re-arranging my life around this endeavour, and in October 1989 *Chiron and the Healing Journey* was published.

## 'BURNISHED INTO THE SOUL'

This exploration continued when a category of newly discovered celestial objects was given the name of 'Centaurs' owing to their orbital similarity with Chiron.[11] In 1994, I heard Richard Tarnas counsel that, 'In astrology, you can only work with what is burnished into your soul.'[12] This aptly described my experience of studying Chiron – and late the following year various events, dreams and synchronicities seemed to indicate that I was once again being called by the Centaurs.[13] On reflection, I have come to feel that this 'burnishing' is also a necessary process without which we cannot really work with the 'normal' planets either.

Students at every stage of their journey of learning will recognise and relish the moment when a planet's energy and meaning suddenly 'comes alive' or 'switches on'. This joyous experience goes beyond book learning and verbal description, essential though these are. Once this has occurred, the experience is never forgotten, like riding a bicycle. To add another banal comparison, studying the planets is like learning to tune in to different radio stations. In this analogy, if you want to know about Saturn in a particular chart, you set your antennae to pick up 'Radio Saturn'! The phrase 'tune in' did not enter the vernacular for no reason, as there is a vibrational reality to its meaning. These are living energies that we work with.

## METALOGUE

This word means 'That which we are speaking about is also arising'[14]. Astrologers know well this intriguing phenomenon, which includes 'that which we are thinking about, or focusing on'. One way we learn about astrology is by watching for displays of the symbolism we are studying, as demonstrated 'live' in our own experiential field. For our purpose, as astrologers, the above definition can also be reversed to say, 'We speak about that which is arising'. Indeed, this is exactly what we do in the consulting situation when describing the astrological counterpart of 'what is arising' in a client's life. The power of 'calling out' the planetary symbolism need never be underestimated, as it is the companion or mirror image of what we call 'interpretation'.

## A MARS METALOGUE

In 2009, in spite of every effort to avoid doing so, I took a long-distance flight on the very day Mars turned retrograde in Leo, squaring my natal Mars in Taurus! I was apprehensive, but curious. After check-in, the fire alarms sounded and the terminal was evacuated. 'Here we go' I thought. 'Mars in a fire sign and Gatwick Airport burns down'. However, after a couple of freezing hours outside with lots of angry (Mars) travellers, we were summarily ushered to the boarding gate. My carefully chosen seat had been changed, but I decided not to make a fuss, given the aspects. Imagine my delight, however, when I was re-directed to the Business Class section. I relished the symbolism, felt suitably Leonine, and tried to adopt the demeanour of one who always travels thus. However, I soon 'retrograded' into humiliation, defeated by the intricacies of the hi-tech environment around my plush seat. I felt like a bewildered Neanderthal (my Mars in Taurus), a hapless participant in an astrological cartoon!

In the midst of this Mars retrograde ineptitude and embarrassment, I became aware of a well-dressed and handsome Indian man, my immediate neighbour. He looked at me with an expression of carefully-veiled amusement, and said 'Can I help?' I was all but helpless with mirth by this time, and gratefully accepted his offer. He pressed the arm-rest between our seats – lo and behold, my tray appeared, as if by magic! Then my benefactor offered tutoring about the 'local technology', which I discovered was not 'rocket science' after all.

The symbolism was breathtaking. Damsel in distress rescued by Mars in Leo hero! Gold cuff-links, expensively dressed, travelling in Business Class, authoritative, kindly, generous. This episode had been a great ice-breaker, and a long conversation developed, deeply imbued with the symbolism of the astrological moment. When asked the 'What do you do?' question, I decided not to lie. Being Indian, I thought this man would surely have at least a cultural familiarity with astrology. His story further elaborated the 'retrograde' symbolism ...

At his birth, the parents of this man, who I will call 'Rajit', received a disturbing prediction from the family astrologer – that their son would die at the age of twenty-eight. That is, unless they arranged for rituals to ward off whatever disaster awaited. So his concerned parents invested a lot of money in this apotropaic process. In due time, Rajit became a fighter pilot in the Indian Air Force. At the age of twenty-six, during active service, an injury ended his career as a fighter pilot, although routine flying was still possible. However, because he 'only ever wanted to be The Best', he explained, unwittingly voicing Mars in Leo, he decided to change career. He started a company manufacturing bionic limbs for amputees, especially war-victims. I almost gasped out loud at the Mars symbolism: war, warrior, heroism, accident, injury, damage, surgery, mobility. And courage. Now I will forever think of Mars retrograde as the soul work of 'turning swords into ploughshares'.

He had a low opinion of astrology. 'You see, I didn't die', he said, somewhat triumphantly, 'and so the prediction wasn't correct'. I pointed out the symbolism – that he did indeed 'die' to the ambitions of his youth, but had undergone a 're-birth' in finding a new life purpose. He became thoughtful, and agreed. Did he believe that the rituals might indeed have saved his life? I asked. He admitted he did not know, adding 'What do you think?' I responded by saying that astrology, whether one 'believes in it' or not, takes us to the edge of the Great Mystery, where there are things that cannot be known in the 'normal' way. And that this can be unnerving.[15]

This illustrates how astrological events may work out quite differently from how we might imagine, fear or predict them, but they *always express the astrological symbolism if we are open to seeing it*. And this is how we learn. It also illustrates 'spontaneous magic', where we do not seek to 'make something happen' but rather we take delight in *what is happening*! Witnessing 'what is arising' has its own power. In the 20th century, quantum mechanics confirmed that the observer is not separate from the scientific experiment, and so affects the outcome. This was not 'news' to astrologers, who had always engaged with planetary energies at a level beyond simple 'push-pull causality'. In this regard, perhaps the delightful metalogue described here served to deflect a negative manifestation of the same energy. Who knows …?

## WORKING IN THE 21ST CENTURY

In my Sufi training I learned about the value of being 'In the world, but not of it', rather than its opposite, 'Being of the world, but not in it'. I believe that we astrologers should neither be subsumed in 'mainstream' culture, nor aloofly rejecting of it. We are the custodians of priceless knowledge, and therefore must be accessible ourselves to share it with others who may need it.[16] However, should this extend into 'astrological evangelism' we run the risk of joining the ranks of those who espouse the secular 'techno-materialism' which dominates our contemporary world. Being 'of that world' may cause our astrology to degrade, withering into superficiality and distraction.

I have been reading charts professionally since 1975, and I can see that the clientele I attract reflect the themes of my own life's journey. Meaning they are often 'under the radar' kind of people, interested in things psychological, metaphysical and philosophical! And often working on illness issues. However, over the last decade I have been fascinated by a new phenomenon in my consulting practice. Clients sometimes arrive with a lot of 'astrological pre-conditioning', developed through surfing the internet and absorbing snippets of information, but without any depth, overview or disciplined framework of study. Astrology has already been mis-used by the client, enlisted in the service of negative or limiting self-concepts and reinforcing them with 'cosmic authority'. Understanding the difference between information, knowledge and wisdom might be a useful consideration — for us astrologers, as well as our clients. Today, astrological information is readily available, but the practice of astrology requires knowledge and wisdom, which in turn require time and commitment lest 'a little knowledge becomes a dangerous thing'.[17]

In 1990, I studied horary astrology with Geoffrey Cornelius, and have used it since; in 2012, I attended Deborah Houlding's 'Practitioner Certificate' course. This surprises many people who think I work mainly with 'weird stuff'![18] However, I relish the interchange between the traditional and the contemporary, and aspire to continue learning in both directions. In the future, I hope that we astrologers will become increasingly discerning about the purpose of what we are doing. Not all approaches or techniques suit all usages at all times. For example, when studying a horary chart, you do not need (at least initially) to engage with the psychological processes so eloquently articulated by the major 20th century astrologers. On the other hand, some of the traditional descriptions of detriment, for example, if mis-applied to a natal chart through lack of psychological understanding, may result in a situation where the client becomes 'afflicted' by the astrologer. There is much to ponder in circumstances such as this.

This apparent contradiction (traditional/psychological) concerns the application of astrological knowledge to the 'outer' and 'inner' worlds respectively. However, in reality, the two overlap and the exchange between opposites is signified by none other than the great Hermes himself, one of our patron gods, who moves deftly around and between them. There are times when a 'translation' into the realm of psychological issues may be necessary to fully 'resolve' a horary chart. Conversely, an apparently 'psychological' issue can sometimes be clarified through the precision of horary. Astrology requires of us a *flexibility of thinking* in order to deepen our ways of understanding its essence and its varied applications. These range from the deep, nuanced, inner processes of spiritual awakening to the literal, concrete, external expressions of personal and historical life-events. As individual astrologers, we place ourselves on this spectrum as befits our own talent, nature and calling, but together we are like a multi-faceted mirror of ever-evolving consciousness.

A LIFE ASTROLOGICAL

## TRIBE, CLAN AND *LINGUA FRANCA*

Our shared symbolic language can transcend national, cultural or racial differences. In addition to tutoring for several major astrological schools in England, I have been fortunate enough to teach in many places abroad where I've seen at first hand the resonance of familiarity between members of the 'astrological tribe'. No matter that we live in different countries, speak different languages, belong to different cultures, generations or astrological schools, we are all doing the same thing: we are inspired by our experience and study of the heavens 'Above', and how their meaning is reflected 'Below'. And we seek to make this knowledge useful to others.

This is an ancient and noble endeavour, and as the *lingua franca* of the Mystery Traditions, astrology is perhaps 'protected'. Meaning that although 'information' may change according to the times we live in, true knowledge never dies out. Rather, the wisdom stream from which it originates perpetually gives rise to new insight and new workings, as we simultaneously gather the harvest from the great souls of the past.

Like any tribe, our astrological one contains many different clans, with different 'totems'. Moreover, these clans do not always agree! It is very difficult for us humans to relinquish the 'need to be right'. However, an unwritten law of esoteric studies is that, knowledge aside, wisdom arises on a 'need to know' basis, to be applied for beneficial purposes, and it may not be hijacked by partisan issues or for personal gain.[19] Cultivating our personal *inner connection to astrology* enables us to learn joyfully from many differing and even conflicting sources: tutors, colleagues, friends and fellow students, writers ancient and modern. Astrology itself will speak as we serve the tradition with diligence, sharing what we see and know – when the situation invites us to do so.

As the journey of writing this piece comes to an end and I reflect on my solitary astrological beginnings in Africa, I feel so grateful to be part of our world-wide community. For, to paraphrase the lyrics of a South African singer-songwriter, we are all 'Scatterlings of the Universe on our journey to the Sun …'[20]

May we, and all those touched by our work, be given guidance, illumination, integrity and compassion as we continue in dedication to our chosen field.

# THE JOURNEY THROUGH ASTROLOGY

## NOTES

1. William Lilly, Alan Leo and Evangeline Adams, for example.

2. Aldous Huxley, *The Perennial Philosophy*, first published in 1945. The term was first used in the 16th century, by Agostino Steuco, who drew on the work of Marsilio Ficino (1433-99) and Pico della Mirandola (1463-94). This demonstrates the influence of astrology on the source of contemporary 'Inter-faith', 'Universalist' and 'Perennialist' beliefs expressed in Huxley's work.

3. 'Universal Declaration of Independence'. Rhodesia severed ties with Britain over the issue of voting rights. A long-drawn out 'bush war' followed, until 1980 when Rhodesia became Zimbabwe.

4. See footnote 2. The 'Western Sufism' of Hazrat Inayat Khan (1882-1927) reveals the same orientation.

5. Colin Evans, ed. Brian E.F. Gardner, *The New Waite's Astrological Compendium* (London: Routledge and Kegan Paul, 1971).

6. The 'Celestial Roots' series, from 1991-94, every summer.

7. Liz Greene, *Saturn: A New Look at an Old Devil* (Maine: Weiser Books, 1976, rev. edn 2001).

8. I recommend the work of Pema Chödrön to clients and students if asked about this.

9. *Hermetic Silence*. Achille Bocchi *Symbolicarum quaestionem de universo genere* (1574).

10. Personal communication, 1987.

11. Melanie Reinhart, *Chiron and the Healing Journey* (London: Starwalker Press, rev. edn 2010), Part I, Chapter 1, p.23-34.

12. Panel discussion at the closing of the Astrological Association annual conference, Canterbury, UK, 1994.

13. The circumstances of this are written up in detail in Melanie Reinhart *Saturn, Chiron and the Centaurs* (London: Starwalker Press, 2011) p. 286-92.

14. Gregory Bateson, *Mind and Nature: A Necessary Unity* (New York: Dutton [Penguin], 1979).

15. See *Comfortable With Uncertainty* by Pema Chödrön, Shambhala reprint, 2004.

16. Epistle to the Astrologer. William Lilly *Christian Astrology* (1647) [hereafter *Christian Astrology*]. Online version annotated by Deborah Houlding http://www.skyscript.co.uk/pdf/CA_preface.pdf> [accessed 28 October 2014], p.24.

17. Alexander Pope *An Essay on Criticism*, 1709 (paraphrased). This appears to be based on a similar passage in *The Mystery of Phanatacism*, written in 1698 by an anonymous author 'A.B.' He in turn mis-quotes Francis Bacon, who said in *The Essays: Of Atheism* (1601): 'A little philosophy inclineth man's mind to atheism; but depth in philosophy bringeth men's mind about to religion.'

18. The newly discovered objects such as Centaurs, Kuiper Belt Objects (KBOs), Trans-Neptunian Objects (TNOs) and Scattered Disk Objects (SDOs).

19. *Christian Astrology*, p.24.

20. Johnny Clegg *Scatterlings of Africa, Juluka* (Warner 23898, unknown medium, 1982). See YouTube for videos of recent performances.

# AUTHORS' BIOGRAPHIES

LAURA ANDRIKOPOULOS MA DFAstrolS is President of the Faculty of Astrological Studies and a tutor on the MA in Cultural Astronomy and Astrology at the Sophia Centre, University of Wales. She is currently pursuing PhD studies in the psychologisation of Western astrology in the 20th century. She is particularly interested in the use of astrology as a spiritual path, enabling the individual to develop a relationship with the cosmos and facilitating insight into one's nature and journey through life. In addition to the Faculty Diploma, she also holds the Katarche Diploma in Horary Astrology from the Company of Astrologers.

DIANE CONWAY BA DFAstrolS holds the Diploma of the Faculty of Astrological Studies, with whom she began her astrological education in 1990. She has also trained in karmic astrology with Judy Hall. Diane is a distance learning tutor for the Faculty and runs an astrological practice in Somerset. Her website is www.dianeconway.co.uk.

DARBY COSTELLO MA Hon DFAstrolS has been an astrologer for more than half her life and is engaged in many layers of the astrological community. She has taught at the CPA since 1988 and lectures and teaches internationally. She has written several books including *The Astrological Moon*, *Water and Fire*, and *Earth and Air*. Darby was awarded the MA in Cultural Astronomy and Astrology at Bath Spa University in 2006. Her first love in astrology is doing charts and her worldwide clientele is the ground from which her astrological inspiration is nourished.

CAT COX MA DFAstrolS began her astrological journey in 1984. Following her training with the Faculty of Astrological Studies where she gained the Diploma in 1996, she completed a traditional horary training with John Frawley in 2003, and was awarded the MA in Cultural Astronomy and Astrology from Bath Spa University in 2007. She is currently the Vice-President and Head Tutor at the Faculty having been a tutor since 2007. Her approach to astrology has been influenced by a long-held interest in the Western Mystery Tradition and in women's spirituality and she has now come to think of her practice as a spiritual practice. Her website is www.starpractice.com.

## AUTHOR'S BIOGRAPHIES

KIM FARLEY DFAstrolS discovered astrology at the end of the 1980s and since then it has enhanced her life in countless ways. She loves the intensity and connection of private consultation work as well as the joy of shared vision experienced in teaching. At the time of writing, she is the longest-serving Faculty class tutor and feels very privileged to have been able to introduce the subject to generations of beginners as well as to encourage and learn from students further down the path. Alongside her private practice and teaching, she has a second vocation as a funeral celebrant.

DEBORAH MORGAN BA DFAstrolS is a practising astrologer based in the United Kingdom. Her practice is informed by her keen interest in the Western Mystery Tradition and the considerable potential of astrology for profound self-development and insight. This is accompanied by parallel interests in the intuitive and philosophical facets of astrology, working with planetary cycles and business astrology. She has fulfilled a variety of roles on the Council of the Faculty of Astrological Studies over the past five years, and is a distance learning tutor for the Faculty.

LINDSAY RADERMACHER MA MPhil DFAstrolS has been part of the UK astrological community since the 1970s, as a teacher, lecturer, member and chair of many of the major astrological organisations and Trusts. She was President of the Faculty (1986-95) and a founder of the APAI. She has an MA from Somerville College, Oxford, and recently completed a postgraduate research degree on the role of dialogue in astrological divination at the University of Kent. Her current focus is working with clients, small group work and supervision – and the sheer enjoyment of a life steeped in astrology. Her practice is in London.

MELANIE REINHART BA DFAstrolS was first introduced to astrology in 1959. She is a patron of the Faculty of Astrological Studies, and received the 2004 Charles Harvey award for 'exceptional service to astrology'. She has taught for many leading astrology schools in the UK and abroad, and runs her own programme of workshops. Her busy consulting practice has an international clientele and is the heart of her work. Melanie's astrology books are published by Starwalker Press and include: *Chiron and the Healing Journey*, *Chiron*, *Saturn and the Centaurs* and *Incarnation*. Her website is www.melaniereinhart.com.

CAROLE TAYLOR BA FFAstrolS is the Faculty's Director of Studies and organiser of its annual Summer School in Oxford. Formerly the President and Head of the London Classes, she has been a Faculty tutor since 2001, both in London and by distance learning. With an interest in complementary health, she spent several years as a reflexologist for the Complementary Health Trust, treating clients with immune-related illnesses. She is studying on the MA in Myth, Cosmology and the Sacred at Canterbury Christ Church University, and runs an astrological practice in West Sussex.

POLLY WALLACE BA DFAstrolS lives in the beautiful Cotswold hills of England. She holds the Diploma of the Faculty of Astrological Studies and an honours degree in English and American Literature. Since 2004 Polly has been a distance learning and Summer School tutor for the Faculty of Astrological Studies. Her articles have been published in various periodicals including *The Mountain Astrologer* and *The Astrological Journal*. Polly is fascinated by how today's astrology, combining ancient wisdom with modern innovation, creates a rich field of ideas to inspire each one of us as our futures unfold.

# BIBLIOGRAPHY

Baez, Fernando *A Universal History of the Destruction of Books: From Ancient Sumer to Modern Iraq* trans. from the Spanish by Alfred MacAdam (London: Atlas and Co, 2008).

Bateson, Gregory *Mind and Nature: A Necessary Unity* (New York: Dutton [Penguin], 1979).

Borges, Jorge Luis lecture entitled *'Poetry'*, from the collection *Seven Nights*, trans. by Eliot Weinberger (New York: New Directions, 2009).

Buber, Martin and Smith, Ronald G. *I and Thou*, 2nd rev. edn (New York: Scribner, 1958).

Buber, Martin and Smith, Ronald G. *Between Man and Man* (London: Kegan Paul 1947).

Cavafy, C.P. Ithaka from C.P. Cavafy *Collected Poems*, trans. by Edmund Keeley and Philip Sherrard (London: Chatto and Windus Limited, 1978).

Campbell, Joseph *Flight of the Wild Gander: Explorations in the Mythological Dimension* (California: New World Library, 2002).

Campbell, Joseph *The Hero with a Thousand Faces* (London: Fontana, 1993).

Chödrön, Pema *Comfortable With Uncertainty* (Shambhala reprint, 2004).

Cornelius, Geoffrey *The Moment of Astrology: Origins in Divination*, rev. edn (Bournemouth: Wessex Astrologer, 2003).

Cornelius, Geoffrey 'Astrology, Imagination, Imaginal', *The Astrological Journal*, Vol.56, No. 1, Jan/Feb 2014.

Costello, Darby The Call of the Spirit: The Training and Practice of Sangomas in Relation to an Astrologer's Vocation, in *Daimonic Imagination: Uncanny Intelligence*, ed. by Angela Voss and William Rowlandson (Cambridge: Cambridge Scholars Publishing, 2013).

Evans, Colin (Gardner, Brian E.F. ed.) *The New Waite's Astrological Compendium* (London: Routledge and Kegan Paul, 1971).

Feaver, Vicki Displaced Art from *Close Relatives: Poems* (London: Martin Secker and Warburg Limited, 1981).

# BIBLIOGRAPHY

Friedman, Maurice S. *Martin Buber: The Life of Dialogue* (London: Routledge and Kegan Paul, 1955).

George, Demetra *Astrology and the Authentic Self: Integrating Traditional and Modern Astrology to Uncover the Essence of the Birth Chart* (Lake Worth, FO: Ibis Press, 2008).

Graves, Robert *The Greek Myths* (Middlesex: Folio Society Edition, 1998).

Greene, Liz *Saturn: A New Look at an Old Devil* (Maine: Weiser Books, 1976, rev. edn 2001).

Greene, Liz and Sharman-Burke, Juliet *The Astrologer, the Counsellor and the Priest* (London: CPA Press, 1997).

Greene, Liz *The Astrology of Fate* (London: Mandala Books, 1985).

Hand, Robert, *Planets in Transit: Life Cycles for Living*, expanded 2nd edn (Atglen, PA: Whitford Press, 2002).

Hanegraaff, Wouter J. 'How Magic Survived the Disenchantment of the World', *Religion*, Vol 33, (2003).

Harvey, Graham *Animism: Respecting the Living World* (London: Hunt & Co, 2005).

Hillman, James *The Soul's Code* (New York: Warner Books, 1996).

Hillman, James 'Heaven Retains Within its Spheres Half of All Bodies and Maladies' (Paracelsus), from *The Alchemical Sky*, James Hillman and Liz Greene (CPA Master Class Series, Astro Logos Ltd, Bristol, 2005).

Holmes, Richard *The Age of Wonder: How the Romantic Generation Discovered the Beauty and Terror of Science* (London: Harper Press, 2009).

Huxley, Aldous *The Perennial Philosophy* (London: Harper Perennial, 2009).

Hyde, Maggie *Jung and Astrology* (London: The Aquarian Press, 1992).

Jung, Carl G., ed, *Man and His Symbols* (London: Picador, 1978).

Jung, Carl G. *Synchronicity: An Acausal Connecting Principle* (London: Routledge and Kegan Paul, 1955).

BIBLIOGRAPHY

Keats, John *On First Looking into Chapman's Homer* anthologised in *Poems on the Underground: Fifth Edition*, ed. by Gerard Benson, Judith Chernaik and Cicely Herbert (London: Cassell Publishers Limited, 1995).

Keats, John *The Letters of John Keats 1814-1821*, 2 vols, ed. H. E. Rollins (Cambridge: Cambridge University Press, 1958).

Landwehr, Joe *The Seven Gates of Soul: Reclaiming the Poetry of Everyday Life* (St. Louis, MO: Ancient Tower Press, 2004), p. 33.

Lévy-Bruhl, Lucien *How Natives Think*, (Princeton: Princeton University Press 1985[1910]).

Luhrmann, Tanya *Persuasion of the Witch's Craft: Ritual Magic in Contemporary England* (Oxford: Blackwell, 1989).

Lewis, C.S. *Prince Caspian – The Return to Narnia* (London: Puffin Books, 1962).

Lewis, C.S. *The Voyage of the Dawn Treader* (London: Puffin Books, 1965).

Lilly, William *Christian Astrology* (Abingdon: Astrology Classics, 2004).

Marks, Tracey *The Astrology of Self-Discovery* (US & Canada: CRCS Publications, 1985).

Martin, Clare *Mapping the Psyche* (London: CPA Press, 2005).

Matthews, Caitlin and John *The Western Way: A Practical guide to the Western Mystery Tradition* (London: Arkana, 1994).

Midgley, Mary *Science as Salvation* (London and New York: Routledge, 1992).

Nagel, Thomas *The View from Nowhere* (Oxford: Oxford University Press, 1986).

Ovid, translated by David Raeburn, *Metamorphoses: A New Verse Translation* (London: Penguin Classics, 2004).

Pope, Alexander *An Essay on Criticism Part II* (London: Penguin Classics, 2011).

Reinhart, Melanie *Chiron and the Healing Journey* (London: Starwalker Press, revised edition 2010).

Reinhart, Melanie *Saturn, Chiron and the Centaurs* (London: Starwalker Press, 2011).

Rilke, Rainer Maria *Letters to a Young Poet*, trans. Stephen Mitchell (New York: Vintage, 1986).

Rudhyar, Dane *The Astrology of Personality* (Sante Fe, NM: Aurora Press, 1991, [1936]).

Tambiah, Stanley *Magic, Science, Religion and the Scope of Rationality* (Cambridge: Cambridge University Press, 1990).

Tarnas, Richard *Cosmos and Psyche, Intimations of a New World View* (New York: Viking, 2006).

Webster, Charles *From Paracelsus to Newton, Magic and the Making of Modern Science* (Cambridge: Cambridge University Press, 1982).

Voss, Angela 'Astrology as Divine Revelation: Some thoughts on Ibn Arabi's Understanding of Imagination', *The Astrological Journal*, Vol. 56, No 6, Nov/Dec 2014.

Willis, Roy and Curry, Patrick *Astrology, Science and Culture: Pulling Down the Moon* (Oxford: Berg, 2004).

# LIST OF ILLUSTRATIONS

The Pre-Modern Cosmos. From Guiart des Moulins, *Bible historiale* (vol. I) Paris, France, 1403-1404. © The British Library Board, Harley 4381 f6v.

Hermes (Attic red-figure vase, c. 480-470 BCE)

The Astrological Glyph for Mercury

Faculty of Astrological Studies, 7 June 1948, 7.50pm, London, UK. Source: Solar Fire

*Fortuna* (Hans Sebald Beham, 1541). Engraving of an allegorical figure representing Fortune (private collection)

*Opera Incompiuta* (William Girometti, 1998: left unfinished because of painter's death) Photo by Silvia Girometti

*Mappa Mundi*. From Jean Mansel's *La Fleur des Histoires*, Valenciennes, 1459-1463 (map attributed to a Simon Marmion). Bibliothèque Royale de Belgique, Bruxelles (MS. 9231, fol. 281v.)

*Mercury and Jupiter in the House of Philemon and Baucis* (Jacob van Oost the Elder). Fine Arts Museum of San Francisco

*A reading woman tries in vain to stop Chronos as he passes by*; representing the inexorable passing of time (stipple engraving, publisher not identified). Wellcome Library, London (Wellcome Library no. 38972i, photo number: V0047955)

*An Astrologer Casting a Horoscope*. From Robert Fludd's *Utriusque Cosmi Historia*, 1617: Universal History Archive/UIG/Bridgeman Images

*Odysseus Departs from the Land of the Phaecians* (Claude Lorrain, 1646). Louvre Museum, Paris

*The Great Library of Alexandria* (Otto von Corvin). Engraving

*Prometheus* (Gustave Moreau, 1868). Musée National Gustave-Moreau, Paris

*Soul in Bondage* (Elihu Vedder, 1891-2). Brooklyn Museum, New York (gift of Mrs. Harold G. Henderson)

My office, 1972-78

The young astrologer and the young sangoma: Ndlaleni Cindi and me, ca. 1973

*Hermetic Silence* (Achille Bocchi, 1574). From *Symbolicarum quaestionem de universo genere* (The Emblems of Achille Bocchi) Plate 64 (engraving 1555), printed by Giulio Bonasone, 1574, Bologna. Getty Research Institute, California

*Finding the point where heaven and earth touch* (Flammarion, 1888). From Camille Flammarion, *L'Atmosphère: Météorologie Populaire* (Librairie Hachette, Paris 1888)

# ABOUT THE FACULTY OF ASTROLOGICAL STUDIES

THE FACULTY OF ASTROLOGICAL STUDIES was founded at 19.50 BST on 7th June 1948 in London, UK. Its aim then and now is to raise the standard of astrological education. Since its establishment, the Faculty has become known worldwide as a first-class astrological teaching body and its Diploma, the DFAstrolS, is among the most highly-valued and recognised international qualifications for the professional astrologer.

Over the years more than 10,000 students from over 90 countries have enrolled on the Faculty's courses, and many of the world's leading astrologers are or were Faculty Diploma holders, such as Liz Greene, Charles Harvey, Julia Parker, Melanie Reinhart and Howard Sasportas. Fellows of the Faculty include Sue Tompkins, Clare Martin and Carole Taylor, and honorary Diploma holders include Rob Hand, Bernard Eccles, Darby Costello and Nick Campion.

The Faculty's courses are comprehensive and flexible, guiding you from the very beginning of your astrological studies right through to professional qualification at Diploma level. You can study by Distance Learning, at Classes in London and at the Faculty's annual Summer School. Details of the Foundation and Diploma course syllabus, the examinations system and our year-round events can be found at www.astrology.org.uk

As a teaching and examining body, the Faculty's team of dedicated, experienced tutors, all of whom hold the Faculty's Diploma, are devoted to teaching astrology to students all over the world.

The Faculty is a Founding Member of the Advisory Panel on Astrological Education, an independent non-profit-making body constituted by the major astrological organisations and teaching bodies in the United Kingdom.

FACULTY PATRONS
Robert Hand, PhD Hon DFAstrolS
Liz Greene PhD DFAstrolS
Baldur Ebertin PhD Hon DFAstrolS
Julia Parker DFAstrolS
Melanie Reinhart BA DFAstrolS

PAST PATRONS
John M Addey MA DFAstrolS
Dane Rudhyar Hon DFAstrolS

Lightning Source UK Ltd.
Milton Keynes UK
UKHW020654140122
397094UK00006B/192